Social Media Marketing Guide 2021

2 Books in 1

Gain Customers Through Instagram, Facebook, Youtube, and Twitter

Daniel Russell

Special Bonus!

Want this book for free?

Get FREE, unlimited access to it and all of my new books by joining the Fan Base!

Scan with Your Camera to Join!

TABLE OF CONTENTS

Instagram Marketing Guide 2021:

Social Media Marketing Guide 2021:

Instagram Marketing Guide 2021

How to Attract Millions of Potential Customers to Your Brand by Using Instagram

INTRODUCTION

As we approach the 28-year anniversary of the availability of the world wide web to the public, it is amazing to reflect on where the internet has taken us since. With LinkedIn's release in 2003, Facebook in 2004, YouTube in 2005, Twitter in 2006, and Pinterest and Instagram in 2010, marketers have been faced with an entirely different set of challenges, and opportunities in reaching their audiences. And with 2 billion users on social platforms combined, it is no wonder that marketers have made social media marketing a priority.

Social media marketing, in the broadest sense, is the process of drumming up attention for your business, through a social media site. And Instagram, is just one of many sites that business marketers are leveraging to help drive conversions and revenue. This list below provides a high-level overview of the various social media sites available today, and the estimated monthly active users.

- Facebook = 2.23 billion monthly active users
- Instagram = 1 billion monthly active users
- LinkedIn = 260 million monthly active users
- Pinterest = 250 million monthly active users
- Snapchat = 300+ million monthly active users
- Twitter = 326 million monthly active users

Determining the correct social media site or sites to engage in with your customers and prospective customers is often a matter of personal or business preference. And, it is often based on the number of users that your business can get in front of. With 59% of people accessing social media at least one time (or more) each day, these sites provide an excellent and convenient way to grow brand awareness for your business.

So, why is social media marketing a must for your company?

1. It is highly likely that your customers are on social media
2. With the prevalence of and preference for social media as a news and information outlet, your customers very likely want to be engaged on one of these sites
3. Social media marketing helps grow brand awareness and authority
4. Social media marketing can help you improve brand loyalty
5. Social media marketing grows inbound traffic (web visits *and* store/location visits)
6. Social media marketing allows you to target and retarget your customers and future customers, but allows you to control frequency to keep interest without creating annoyance
7. Social media marketing is much more cost-effective than many of the more traditional channels
8. Social media marketing can help you improve your rankings with various search engines
9. Your competition is definitely on social media
10. Social media marketing is proven to lead to increased conversation rates

11. Consumers like to see (and follow) recommendations that are provided to them on social media
12. Social media marketing can help you grow your customer base
13. Social media sites often provide insight capabilities for businesses so that they can learn more about their customers

When your business engages with social media and pays attention to what your customers and potential customers are doing and saying, you gain insights into what they care about. This provides you with the ability to solve for your customer's challenges and concerns, as well as understand what they want to see, so that you can tailor your content accordingly. These actions on the part of your business will have an inevitable positive result on customer service and your customers perceptions of you.

In this book, we will focus on Instagram as a key site for your business to engage. With Instagram in particular, there are over 1 billion users on Instagram, with 500 million of those engaging in some sort of daily activity. The impressive statistics don't stop there. It is estimated that 100+ million photos and videos are posted each and every day, and 50 billion photos shared to date. That's a pretty compelling statistic to indicate that people are paying attention. In fact, users are generating 4.2 billion likes per day!

If your customers are on Instagram, your business needs to be too. And 25 million businesses have already created accounts and started developing compelling strategies to engage with their customers. It's easy to connect with your customers where they are, and today, social media is the place. Consider these facts:

- Online adults aged 18 - 34 are most likely to follow a brand via social networking

- 60% of users seek out and discover new products on Instagram
- 71% of US businesses use Instagram
- There are over 25 million active business accounts on Instagram
- There are 2 million monthly advertisers on Instagram
- 60% of users discover products on Instagram

If those statistics aren't impressive enough, keep reading. Remember that Instagram was and is a photo-sharing application. This means that users are sharing their experiences with not just words, but with engaging photos that draw in other visitors who want to learn more. If you're a business with a website or even an old-school product catalog from the days before technology took over, you likely show some sort of photo or other graphical depiction to portray the product you have available. This is because people want to see what it is they are buying before they buy it.

Photos and videos play a substantial role in getting customers to convert; to turn their search and browse behavior into action or conversion. And that's what all marketers are trying to do - drive conversions.

Dispelling the misconceptions about Instagram marketing

Even though social media marketing has become a mainstay for all marketers, there still remain some misconceptions, which I will dispel here.

1. All social media platforms are the same - This is absolutely not the case as each social media platform was created for a particular purpose. In the instance of Instagram, it is to elicit excitement and interest through the use of engaging imagery.
2. Marketers need a presence on all social media channels - While I don't suggest putting all of your eggs in one basket and you will learn in this guide about the benefits of integration with Facebook, it is not necessary for you to be on all channels, especially if you do not have the resources to manage content consistently.
3. Social media is for younger people - While it is true that use varies by age, it is also true that all age groups have a representation on social media.88% of 18-29-year-olds use social media, as does 78% of Americans age 30-49, 64% of Americans age 50-64, and 37% of Americans age 65+.
4. Social media doesn't have a role in all industries - This couldn't be further from the truth. Social media provides a mechanism for any industry to gain brand awareness, whether selling a product or service, or just to put thought leadership on your industry and relevant learnings out into the market.
5. Social media is free - It is true that you can set up a social media account at no cost. However, social media advertising, content development, imagery production, etc., can all come at a cost, especially when looking to generate content of high-quality.
6. Social media can't be measured - At this point, most social media channels have begun offering insight tools that can aid in measurement of clicks, read-through, and a variety of other key performance indicators (KPIs).

7. It's all about the hashtags - We'll spend time reviewing the hashtag strategy later in this guide. And hashtags are important. However, it is possible to overdo it, so remember that the hashtag strategy is all about relevance, connection, organization, and balance.
8. Social media is time consuming - Indeed it can be. But, it is also the cheapest form of advertising available. You can gain exposure to over 1,000 people, for less than the cost of a cup of your favorite Starbucks beverage.
9. Negative comments are bad for your business - Yes, negative word of mouth can have unfortunate ramifications, but research shows that companies that engage with their unsatisfied (and satisfied) customers gain more loyalty and repeat transactions than those that do not.
10. Your competition will always be a step ahead of you - If you don't have a social media presence and they do, yes, you are behind. But by reading this guide and taking our suggestions and implementing them in your business, you will have the opportunity to not only catch up, but also hopefully outshine.
11. It doesn't matter how often I post as long as I am sure to post sometimes - You'll learn in this guide that frequency is important, but so too is consistency. Your customers will be looking for predictability, and you can also leverage time of day and day of week suggestions to ensure you are maximizing your brand exposure.
12. Social media marketing is a fad that will pass by soon - Word of mouth marketing has played a role for decades, and since social media presents a forum for users to share their opinions, it is highly unlikely that it will go away anytime soon.

13. I can stick to traditional marketing and be just as successful - As social media provides the best mechanism today to build brand awareness and provides some of the best reach available, it would be very unfortunate for any marketer to pass this opportunity by.

In this book, I'll provide you with the steps you need to start using Instagram successfully in your business. Let's dive into:

- Introduction to Instagram basics
- Identifying your goals and objectives
- Setting up your Instagram business profile
- Understanding your niche
- How to start posting high-quality content
- Tips on getting new followers
- How to use hashtags
- The several secret tips of Instagram marketing
- Developing an influencer strategy
- Best time of day and day of week to engage and post

After reading this guide, I promise that you will be more informed and better equipped to develop an Instagram marketing strategy for your business. If you don't have a presence on Instagram or other social sites yet, the time to start is right now. Better yet, this guide has been designed to provide just the right level of detail to get you started, and the intuitive userface provided by Instagram will help you learn even more as you go.

So what are you waiting for? Read on and start improving your customer engagement today.

CHAPTER 1

INTRODUCTION TO INSTAGRAM BASICS

Instagram marketing has become a core strategy for any modern day marketer. With such a massive and diverse audience, the platform makes it easy for marketers to get in front of existing customers to drive loyalty and repeat purchases, and to new customers to build brand awareness and interest, with the hopes of driving them to their website to make a purchase. And with the recent release of Instagram shopping, it is now easier than ever for consumers to make their transaction, right on the Instagram site, but more on that later. To that end, Instagram has done a fantastic job of innovating to increase usability and relevance for users.

Instagram provides an easy to use and sleek interface, that even the most novice of technology-users can figure out after just a short time. And since Instagram users are incredibly engaged, and more so than on other platforms, it supports the belief that Instagram is quite simple and easy to use.

You don't have to sell products on eCommerce to have a presence on Instagram

If you just starting reading through this guide and are thinking that your business isn't an eCommerce business and so Instagram isn't the place for you, think again. Remember, the key proposition that Instagram brings is visualization. Consider these examples:

1. You're a real estate agent and want to highlight the newest mountain home that you have on the market
2. You are a world-class hospital that just released a new mother's ward with beautiful birthing and stay suites with a spa-like feel
3. You're a restaurant owner and want to highlight your savory and mouthwatering specials each week

The above examples are all situations where nothing is actually being transacted online, but the business is building brand awareness and drumming up interest so that the consumer will visit their website, or pick up the phone, to learn more.

The mysterious Instagram algorithm

While we'll never know exactly how Instagram has weighted the various data points that they put into their algorithm, we do know that Instagram's back-end technology now focuses on relevancy, serving up the posts that are most likely to relate to certain users based on their activity on the site. So, every time a user clicks through a post, or spends a certain amount of time looking at a certain influencer, Instagram is capturing that data in some way, and building it into their engine to ensure that posts that users won't care about are less likely to show up in their feed.

We do know, however, that Instagram is looking at the following:

- Timely content - This is all about recency, meaning if a user hasn't logged in for a while, they won't have to scroll through outdated (and no longer relevant) posts. They'll be shown timely content that matters to them.
- Interest - This is really the secret sauce, as Instagram is *paying attention*, and will serve content that it believes the user will be interested in.
- Relationships - Instagram knows what photos users tag, and where they comment. So, if a user has interacted in some way with certain brands in the past, they are far more likely to be served content from that brand, or similar brands, in the future.

For marketers, this is a great thing. It means that as Instagram learns more about your brand, your posts and advertisements are more likely to get in front of your niche, or target audience.

Be sure to make note of this insight into Instagram's algorithm when reviewing chapter 10 later in this Instagram Marketing guide when we further explore the best time of day and days of the week to share content.

A few notes about Instagram Shopping

With the release of Instagram Shopping in late 2016, Instagram literally turned their platform into an online marketplace. While it is still a common practice to include website links to your business site, and even to a product page, now it is possible to allow the customer to transact directly on the Instagram platform. For businesses that want to enable the Shopping capability, they need to meet the following requirements:

- You must have an Instagram business profile

- That business profile needs to be connected to a Facebook catalog
- Your company's registered headquarters location must be located in one of the Instagram approved countries
- Items for sale must be physical goods that comply with the trading guideline and terms of use set forth by Instagram

As this Guide is intended as a resource for those getting started with Instagram marketing, I will not be providing a deep dive of the Instagram Shopping capability. However, as your business becomes more mature in your social media strategies, keep this option in mind as a future iteration of what you offer.

CHAPTER 2

IDENTIFYING YOUR GOALS AND OBJECTIVES

To be successful with any social media marketing program, you need to start by identifying your goals and objectives. Typically, goals will address these questions:

- Are you trying to build brand awareness?
- Are you trying to showcase your products and services?
- Is there already an engaged community that you wish to grow?
- Do you want to increase brand loyalty?
- Are you looking to educate your customers and future customers on some topic?

Here are some typical goals that other marketers measure on Instagram:

- Improve your storytelling efforts
- Increase audience engagement

- Increase product sales
- Drive traffic to your website
- Convert people to your email list
- Connect with influencers in your niche
- Share your company culture
- Build momentum and awareness for an upcoming product launch

Now that you have thought through these above questions and have established the goals and objectives that are important to you and your business at a high level, you are ready to define them to make them more specific and actionable.

Identify your target audience

If you have not already established your target audience, then one of the first steps to do this is to figure out who you are selling to. A key place to start is by understanding their core demographics, such as:

- Gender or orientation
- Presence of children
- Marital status
- Geographical location
- Age
- Income level
- Education status
- Working situation
- Housing situation (if applicable to your product)
- Religion (if applicable to your product)

Once you understand the above, you can work on the development of your customer persona. In some cases, you will have more than one persona. The difference between your customer persona(s) and your target audience is that the persona establishes what is unique about the groupings of customers within the target audience.

Here is an example of different personas that one might have for an online bookseller.

- Persona 1 = Female, has children, married, lives in suburbs, age between 30 - 49, household income greater than $100k, has a bachelors degree, stay at home mom, owns home, buys one to three books per month
- Persona 2 = Female, does not have children, not married, lives in city, age between 20 - 29, household income greater than $150k, has a masters degree, executive, rents and apartment, buys one to three books per year
- Persona 3 = Male, has children, married, lives in suburbs, age between 30 - 49, household income greater than $100k, has a masters degree, executive, owns home, buys six books per year
- Persona 4 = Male, does not have children, not married, lives in city, age between 20 - 29, household income less than $100k, in college, part time job/student, lives with parents, no data found on book purchases online

Each of the above personas has varying backgrounds and interests, even though some of their demographics are similar. One or more of these customers might be perfect for you, but the others, in this case, Persona 4 for our example, isn't worth focusing your marketing dollars and time on, because he is not nearly as interested in the types of books that you sell.

Now that we have identified the four personas for our online bookseller business, we can think about how to relate those personas to our brand. Let's say that this bookseller caters to young families with children. They sell your typical book genres including dramas and romance, mystery, horror, and also have a deep assortment of children's books. I believe that Persona 1 and 3 are an excellent target for our core selection of products. However, occasionally the bookseller releases a self-improvement book that is tailored to those in senior positions within their careers. In this case, those books would resonate with Personas 2 and 3. And then on other occasions, the bookseller releases a book for parents with college-aged children, or those preparing to send their children off to college. In this case, those books would likely resonate with Personas 1 and 3, and maybe a little bit of Persona 4.

For this particular bookseller, there is a need to tailor messaging about their products based on the interests of their different personas.

When developing your personas, you want to start simple with core demographics such as age and gender, and then start getting more detailed with the other demographics that I listed above. For those looking to build more sophisticated personas, looking at psychographic data is the next step. In this case, you are looking at a person's values, attributes, and interests. So if you knew that Persona 1 loved mystery and romance novels and purchased on average, one to three books per *month*, you would know that you'd want to target her much more frequently than Persona 2, who maybe buys one to three mystery and romance novels per *year*.

Let's break down Persona 1 just a bit further so that we can better visualize how deep we can get. First, we see the basic information we know about Persona 1. Then, we see the additional information that we can layer in about her, to help us get more granular in the messaging we want to put in front of her.

Persona 1 - Core Demographics

1. Female
2. Has children
3. Married
4. Live in suburbs
5. Age 30 - 49
6. Household income greater than $100k
7. Has a bachelor's degree
8. Stay at home mom
9. Owns a home

Persona 1 - Additional Psychographic Information

1. Plans to go back to work at a law firm once her youngest child starts primary school
2. Loves traveling internationally
3. Worked full-time until her first child was born
4. Has a degree in business administration and earned her paralegal degree
5. Used to work as a paralegal for a small law firm

With just these additional psychographic details, we know much more about Persona 1. We can deduce that she is well-educated and has big goals, both to get back into the workplace and to travel internationally. Now that we know this about her, we may want to consider targeting her for similar books as we targeted to Personas 2 and 3, as we know that Persona 1 is also career-minded.

Going back to the notion of adding psychographics, we can get a glimpse into the person's skills, how much time he or she spends online each week, where they like to shop, the cars they drive, and much more.For those businesses wanting to develop a truly deep understanding of their customers, there are a variety of data firms that can help do just that.

Now that you understand your personas, you can begin applying those personas to your marketing strategy. When done correctly, incorporation of your personas into your strategy will help you drive greater conversions rates, thus improving your return on investment (ROI).

As a reminder, your customer personas are not the same as your target market. Rather, they are a way of digging deeper into the type of potential buyers that you have within that target market.

Your marketing strategy should be built to focus on those customers who fit your ideal persona and that will find your brand relevant. The more you can learn about their age, job, income, geographic location, and living situation, the smarter you will be. And if you can layer in those psychographics details, you can deliver much more personalized campaigns.

CHAPTER 3

SETTING UP YOUR INSTAGRAM BUSINESS PROFILE

If you're a new marketer (or business owner) to Instagram, follow these steps to set up your business profile.

1. Download the app on your mobile device, and save the Instagram website to your favorites or places on your laptop or notebook. The Instagram app is available for smartphones and computers of all kinds through your applicable apps or online store. As the app is really built for use on a mobile device, and you just never know when a great bit of content might be worthy of interaction, having the ability to monitor and post on behalf of your company via a mobile device is a critical necessity. Just note that some of the features available to you on your mobile device will not be available on your computer, or will require certain plug-ins. Because of the laptop limitations, our guide will primarily focus on how to set up your business account via a mobile app.

2. Create your account by either signing in with your email address or phone number and entering a user name, or by logging in with the same information from your business Facebook page. If your business does not have a Facebook page, I highly recommend that you pursue the development of one. Instagram also provides some easy to follow steps to connect your Instagram account here in their Help Center.

3. Complete the profile set-up by entering your email address, phone number, and the physical address for your business. Some information may auto-fill for you from your Facebook account, but Instagram will not allow you to proceed without entering some or all of this information if the fields are blank. Once you have entered the requested information, click on "Done" and then go to your profile. If you have a personal Instagram account, you will be able to access either account from your device by paying attention to the user name listed at the top of the mobile browser. Be sure that any time you are posting on behalf of your business, that your business name appears. But don't worry, if you accidentally post from the wrong account, it is possible to go in and delete the erroneous post.

4. Create your new business page if you haven't already created your Facebook business page. Select a title for your page (most likely your business or company name) and then select the category that best represents the type of business you are in. For example, you will be able to select from:

- Books & Magazines
- Brands & Products
- Companies & Organizations
- Event Sources

- Local Businesses
- Movies
- Music
- Other
- People
- Sports
- Television
- Websites & Blogs

After selecting your primary category, you will need to select a subcategory, and the subcategories will vary based on the primary category that you select. Your subcategory is what will help you drill down into your actual business, such as Nail Salon.

5. Edit your profile by returning to your profile page. Add a photo, a company bio which should include a description of your business using brand language as well as any important links or hashtags, and finally, a link to your website. If you are a business marketer, it is important that you use your company's primary logo here (or an app-based version of the logo) so that customers can leverage their brand recognition that already exists, or can build association the more that they get to know your brand.

A quick note on the importance of your bio. You need to make sure it is both clear and succinct so that users understand what your business does, and can then make a decision on whether or not they want to follow you. Right below your bio should be the link to the landing page of your website. This link is an aid to your call to action, in that it shows users where to go to learn more.

Also, while you will learn more about hashtags in a later chapter, know that you can add clickable hashtags to your bio, which will help you get more visits to your website.

6. Create connections. For a business, a great place to start is by connecting to other users at your place of work and then asking them to create additional connections for the brand. The more users you can get to follow your brand, the better and quicker you will be able to build credibility and get more and more users to see your posts.
7. Add images and video content to your gallery. Even though you may launch more formal campaigns later, it is important to fill your gallery with a core set of imagery that reflects your brand now. You can click on the plus sign to add photos. A great follow-on step at this point is to set up Instagram Stories to drive engagement. Similar to SnapChat's approach, Instagram Stories consists of photo and video content that lives on the platform for only 24 hours. See more about how to post your Instagram Story in chapter 8.

CHAPTER 4

UNDERSTANDING YOUR NICHE

Before we dive into the importance of a niche when it comes to Instagram marketing, let's first ensure you understand the difference between a niche and your target market or audience. A niche defines the service or products that you specialize in, and want to advertise to your potential buyers. Your target market is those potential buyers that are hopefully interested in your niche.

Understanding your target market is important because you need to understand where to find them so that you can develop your marketing strategy, and so that your market will understand that your offerings are dedicated to them and their interests. Further, your target market will already have networks of communication in place, as it is a market, and not just an individual. This means that those within your market are likely interacting with one another and with many of the same modes of communication available to them such as magazines, social forums, etc.

The niche is then your area of specialization that you want to be known for. Often, this means you are leveraging some form of differentiation that sets you apart from other service providers or manufacturers or businesses that offer something similar to your product or service.

Understanding how you are different from other providers is critical to defining your niche. Generally, your differentiator must be true and important to your potential customers. Further, you need to be able to prove it. You can't just say that you are different because your customers will expect you to be able to tell them *how* you are different.

If you're not sure of your niche, consider these questions below to narrow it down.

1. Write down your businesses interests and passions. How and why did your company get its start?

2. What are the business problems for others that you are trying to solve? What conversations have you had with your target market to date, and what have they told you?

3. Who is your competition? How long have they been in business and how did they get their start? What does their marketing content look like? Do they have a presence on Instagram or other social media platforms? How many followers do they have and what do those followers, as a general group, look like?

4. Is your perceived niche profitable? If people don't actually want to solve their business problem, then you won't be able to generate revenue. And if your target market is incredibly small, and your product or services are a one-time need, then it may be difficult to make money long term. Your goal here is to ensure that your niche will be profitable for years to come.

5. Have you tested your idea, live in the market? This is different than the initial focus group testing that you need during the product development phase. Rather, this is about testing your finished product

by setting up your company website and driving traffic to your site with paid advertising tactics. If people aren't coming to your site, what type of A/B testing have you done to play with various subject lines, offers, etc., to see what best resonates?

CHAPTER 5

HOW TO START POSTING HIGH-QUALITY CONTENT

At this point, your Instagram account is set up, you have identified your target market and your personas, and you understand your niche. The next step is to being posting high-quality content that will resonate with your prospective buyers (your target market).

When you think about the content you wish to create, you need to remember that content marketing is all about delivering relevant and quality information to your target audience. Then, within your content strategy, you need to think about context, which is ensuring you are delivering the right information to the right audience at the right time. Therefore, consider these elements of your story, within the applicable context:

- **Who** do you wish to deliver the content to?
- **Where** will your audience consume the content? (In this case, via the Instagram platform)

- **When** will your content be delivered (see more on this in chapter 10)?
- **Why** will this content be important or interesting to your audience?
- **What** kind of content do you wish to create?

Before posting just any content, remember that Instagram was developed as a photo sharing site, and not just any photo sharing site. The site is trendy and the majority of the photos you will see on the site are of very high quality. The site is a great place to show off your photography talents, and many users do just that. Even celebrities across all industries are using Instagram to share their photos, and as part of an influencer strategy (more on that later).

So, now is not the time to cut costs or corners if you can avoid it (though we will touch on some options later on how to take your own photos). With over 25 million businesses on Instagram, your competition is likely already engaging followers, and if they aren't yet, they will be soon (they may even be reading this Instagram Marketing Guide right now, just like you).

Here are some quick tips on how to produce high-quality content:

1. You don't have to be a Photoshop whiz, but if you are fortunate enough to have a creative or art director on your marketing team, this is likely a task to offload to that individual. They will likely be well versed in the tips and tricks to developing Instagram content. And if they are not, share these quick tips with them, and they will likely be able to whip you up something magical in no time. But, if you are not that fortunate and you are a team of one, then know that there are a variety of templates available to you, to help you create your content.

Online design tools such as Canva, Creative Market, and PicMonkey have done the hard work for you, and have developed a variety of templates that are available for purchase, for a nominal fee. So, find the templates that work the best for your brand, and then stick with them. Consistency here is key.

2. If you don't have the creative talent in-house, then you will likely need to set up your own photo studio to take some relevant product photos or invest in high-quality stock photography. Shutterstock and Getty Images are common go-tos, but if you are looking for something a bit more unique, try Unsplash or Stocksy.

3. Don't think that professional photography or stock imagery are your only options. With iPhone and smartphone technology improving all the time, you can actually take some amazing photos with your mobile device. And remember that your followers are users too, and they are likely taking photos in the same way.

4. When taking your own images, be sure to stick to one subject, and use the rule of thirds for more captivating and intriguing photos. If your camera has the ability to show gridlines in your viewfinder, then this is an easy approach. If not, simply eyeball it and place your photo subject at the intersection of one of the sets of lines so that the image is in one-third of the photo, and not necessarily the center.

In many cases, you will have to do some editing to make your photo Instagram worthy. In most cases, those amazing photos you see on other feeds were not simply one and done. Luckily for you, Instagram provides a variety of built-in filters and other tools that will make it very easy for you to edit your photos. And, there are a plethora of other apps available for download that can create some fun final products.

Some favorite apps are Facetune, Perfect365 (great for slimming down your subjects and removing blemishes), Image Blender, Retouch, Photoshop Mix, Color Effects, and Color Changer.

5. Avoid using the same format over and over. Some users will respond to certain formats more than others, so be sure to experience with both static imagery as well as videos. The goal here is to engage the audience and video content viewership is on the rise. Take a look at these quick stats:

- 55% of people watch videos online every day
- 92% of mobile video consumers share videos with others
- 90% of users say that product videos are helpful in the decision process, and after watching a video, 64% of users are more likely to buy a product online
- Social video generates 1200% more shares than text and images combined
- 80% of users recall a video ad they viewed in the past 30 days

So, understanding that video is very important to social media consumption these days, make sure too that video is not your only approach. A high-quality content strategy is very much about balance. But this also doesn't mean you only have certain static photos and certain videos... be sure to mix it up. Your video content can consist of tutorials (how-tos), product introductions and overviews, or simply a public service message that your company might feel strong about (think about a public reaction to a recent tragedy in the news).

Many users do keep their phones on silent as they often check their feeds at work or in other places where they might want to be discreet. Additionally, Instagram defaults to playing videos with no sound. So, if you have sound on your video, you should ensure that the first three seconds or so don't require sound, and you may want to consider adding a caption to the video to tell your viewers to turn on their sound for a better viewing experience.

Instagram also provides you with the ability to take photos directly in the app, which is very convenient (but don't forget our advice on editing). One cool feature that the Instagram in-app camera provides is the Boomerang setting. This setting takes three-second videos that loop, creating a "mini-video." This gives you the opportunity to use a burst of photos and then stitch them together to make a short video. Try this for active situations such as a fist-bump, jumping, or other such activity.

6. GIFs are a fun approach as well and can help create variety in your strategy. GIFs create humor and are easy for your users to consume, and provide a nice "in between" approach as they are not static like an image, and are not as long in length as a video.

GIFs help to keep your social media profile on trend and interesting and further, they help you to connect with users in a new way due to their ability to evoke emotion. GIFs also have a very high tendency to go viral which is an added bonus when you are trying to gain more and more followers.

7. Don't be afraid to share content from other profiles that are within your niche. As long as you ask permission and provide credit for whatever you are using, this is a great practice when you don't have time to create enough of your own content. Just make sure that this is not your only approach. To repost Instagram content, and do it in a way that keeps you out of trouble, follow this approach:

8. Search for other Instagram profiles that resonate with you and your niche. Make note of those profiles and start following them.

9. When you find a post that you think is worthy of a share with your own followers, simply send a direct message (via Instagram) to the content owner, and ask for permission to share the post on your feed.
10. Once you are authorized to do so, go ahead and share the content. To do this, simply click on the image and save it as a JPEG in your own files. Then, upload the photo your feed with your original caption that refers to the original account and tags them in the process.
11. Consider running a campaign that is created with user-generated content (UGC). A great example of this was the Coca-Cola strategy of a few years back with their "Share a Coke" campaign tied to their personalized bottles. This campaign took off like crazy as users shared photos of themselves enjoying a cold Coca-Cola in various places all over the world, with their name emblazoned on the bottle. This campaign promoted millions of revenue and created an entirely new and personalized image for the Coca-Cola brand.

So we understand that not every company can be Coca-Cola or have the resources to personalize a product with every name in the world. But, let's go back to that online bookseller that I talked about in a previous chapter. Consider former First Lady Michelle Obama's book, titled "Becoming Michelle Obama." Think of the impact of a campaign targeted towards other like-minded women, that encourages these women to share photos of them with the book, anywhere and everywhere that they might be reading. Not only is this fun for your readers, but it creates interest and an ability to relate to other users, and on top of that, it creates demand for the book, which is great for your business as a reseller.

12. Develop an influencer strategy. While this will be discussed in more detail in chapter 9, it's important

to know that an influencer strategy is one where a marketer relies heavily (but not primarily) on others to aid in building brand awareness, building authority, and connecting with more users.

Now that you have read through the various tips to create high-quality content, the next step is to begin experimenting with different options. It will take you some time to review the various templates that are available, and decide if you want to take a stock imagery approach, or if you want to go it solo with your iPhone or digital camera. Whatever approach you decide, keep quality at the top of your mind. And, as you move forward, pay attention to what resonates with your audience and what does not, and allow yourself to evolve. By staying attuned to what your audience is looking for, it will be far easier for you to maintain your existing follower base and gain new ones.

CHAPTER 6

HOW TO USE HASHTAGS

So, let's make sure you understand what hashtags are, as these are critical in helping you to stay on trend and to grow your followers.

Hashtags leverage keywords or phrases that are placed together without spaces and then are preferred with that # symbol. In most cases, they are used to reference events, key goings-on in the entertainment industry, or recurring themes.

Hashtags were made popular by Twitter, but it is interesting to note that when Twitter launched in 2006, it didn't have any hashtags (yet). And actually, the @ symbol came first, just eight months after the now-popular platform went live. The first use of this symbol is believed to have been by Robert S. Anderson, the founding designer for Square.

The first use of the # came from Chris Messina (not the actor) who is known as an advocate for open-source software. In August 2007, he proposed the use of the hashtag as a way to add organization to tweets. It didn't take long for the concept to take off, and in July 2009, the hashtag was made an official feature. Facebook followed in 2013.

Development of your hashtag strategy is critical to creating engagement with your followers. In fact, it is believed that the use of a hashtag will increase engagement by more than 10%. Effective use of a hashtag can and will help you to increase your followers.

Every post can have up to 30 hashtags, and when using the right hashtags, it will enable users to find your content more easily. So, in our repeated illustration of the online bookseller, consider posts that add #bestbooksinbrooklyn (if our bookseller is located in Brooklyn), #amreading, #booklovers, #bibliophile, #bookaddict, #books, #bookshelf, and so on and so forth. You get the picture (pun intended).

An additional benefit of your new Instagram business account is the ability to analyze the effectiveness of your hashtags, to see the number of impressions you are getting. This is great information to help ensure you are using the right hashtags in your Instagram strategy. To see this data, simply open one of your posts and select the "View Insights" text below it.

As of 2018, users can also follow hashtags, just like they can another user, which can help you to stay current on topics and communities that are relevant to your interests. And there are a variety of different styles of hashtags, based on what you are trying to accomplish.

- Branded hashtags are specific to your company and could be your company name or a tagline.
- Community hashtags are intended to connect users around a specific subject and similar interests. The #amreading and #booklovers hashtags mentioned above are great examples as they indirectly refer to your brand in that they are about books and reading, but directly tie to the interest of reading itself.

- Campaign hashtags are used for a specific campaign, and only for a short duration of time. So, if our online bookseller issued a reading challenge, a suitable hashtag might be #2021readingchallenge.

Be careful when developing your hashtags to now get too general. While the #books hashtag works, it is pretty broad, and at the time of this writing, there were 35,786,067 Instagram posts using this hashtag. So, look for or develop hashtags that better tie to your niche. A great way to do this is by looking at what hashtags your audience and competitors are already using.

Also, check what hashtags your influencers (or ideal influencers) are using. Since these people are spokespersons for various industries, they are viewed as experts in the space, and perform well on social media, partially due to how and what hashtags they use to draw in more and more followers.

CHAPTER 7

TIPS ON GETTING NEW FOLLOWERS

When you first get started on Instagram, understand that it will take some time before you start seeing followers and any engagement or activity. If you see something immediately, consider this to be luck. As with any marketing program, it takes time to generate interest and build brand awareness.

That said, there are many ways that you can increase your volume of followers.

1. Use those hashtags and use popular hashtags so that your images get found in search. Consider creating a branded hashtag and then encourage your followers to use it.
2. Like photos from others in your target audience.
3. Hold an Instagram contest.
4. Use your other social media accounts to inform others of your Instagram account

5. Understand what time of day that posts are most effective. Research shows that posts at 2AM or 5PM strongly resonate.
6. Follow other users who are using popular hashtags like #followme and #likeforlike - you may find that they will follow you back.
7. Quality is more important than quantity.
8. Create engagement by asking questions or using calls to action in your content.
9. While it may seem counter-intuitive, consider posting some of your content on Sundays when Instagram is less active. This might actually get your more visibility.
10. Explore the use of geo-tagging so that you can capture the attention of local users.
11. Use a tool like PicFrame to combine up to nine photos or videos for one post.
12. Leverage an influencer strategy (refer to chapter 9 for more information).
13. Use faces in your photos.
14. Tag people in your photos when relevant. This ensures those photos show up in those users' feeds, and makes it more likely they'll share them.
15. Share user-generated images.
16. Promote your Instagram username on your physical marketing materials, and if you host an event, encourage attendees to post at your event and include your username and branded event hashtag.
17. Post images with quotes such as motivational, inspirational, or humorous quotes.

CHAPTER 8

SEVERAL SECRET TIPS OF INSTAGRAM MARKETING

Now that you have learned how to set up your account and how to develop an Instagram marketing strategy, it's a good time to provide a punch list of key information that any marketer needs to know to be successful.

First, let's discuss the types of Instagram posts.

1. While I discussed the importance of images and videos previously in Chapter 5, I need to reiterate that you need to share a variety of photos, and those photos need to be of high quality. Your users will be seeking genuine content from your brand, and don't just want to see advertisements. So, think out of the box and capture images of your products, but also your company culture with behind-the-scenes shots. People like to see photos of other people, so this is a great opportunity to showcase your people having fun at work. Remember that people like to buy from companies that treat their employees well, that do good things for the environment, etc.

Sticking to the topic of images, make sure you are using high-resolution photos on your feed, and remember that no matter what size image you share, they will portray as squares on your feed.

- Square images should be 1080 x 1080 pixels
- Landscape images should be 1080 x 566 pixels
- Profile images should be 1350 x 1080 pixels

2. Don't be afraid to share content from your employees. This is a great way to curate authentic content that shows the human side of your company. This will help your audience engage with your brand and feel better about doing business with you.

Content showcasing your people at work is very people-centric, and your followers will love getting an insider's glimpse into your business. Here are a few ideas to help you think through a strategy for this employee-focused content:

- Showing candid photos of your employees at work (ensure your photos don't capture anything that shouldn't be shared with the public such as confidential information).
- Your employees outside of work, perhaps at a community event or even at a happy hour, as long as you don't show anything in the photo that you don't want the public to see. Team-building activities are a great source of imagery and related messaging.
- Showcase pets at work if you have a take your pet to work day.
- Showcase children participating in an event at your workplace on take your child to work day. In these cases, ensure permission from parents, or take photos in a way that doesn't show their faces directly.

3. Be sure to show your humanity. While I never want anything bad to happen, sometimes things do happen. In times of tragedy or crises, show your followers that you are there for them and that their well-being is more important than selling your product.
4. Play up the holidays... all of them. This isn't just about your typical holidays such as Christmas, or Easter, or Mother's Day, or Father's Day. Think about those unique holidays such as National Siblings Day... capture a great photo of one of your employees doing something special with their sibling that day and turn that into content. If your company practices green strategies, be sure to capture those actions on film and share them on Earth Day. Look for those unique opportunities to participate in the stories that captivate others.
5. Utilize the Instagram Stories capability. As a reminder, this feature enables users to post more frequently without bogging down your feed. Stories are intended to be more organic, both for photos and videos, and these posts will disappear after just 24 hours. To post on Your Story, simply select the circle on the top of your screen that says Your Story. Then, you can take your photo.

You'll notice that when in the camera function, there are several options listed at the bottom. Here is what each of them means:

- **Type** - This allows you to type verbiage that will appear on top of your photo
- **Music** - This allows you to add a music clip to one of your images or videos
- **Live** - This allows you to take a video and publish it live to your followers to watch (see more information on this below)

- **Normal** - This is your standard camera function
- Boomerang – I mentioned this previously, but this allows you to take three-second videos that loop, creating a "mini-video"
- Superzoom - This creates an animated zoom
- Focus - Blurs your background to provide emphasis to your main subject
- Remind - Allows you to play your videos in reverse
- Hands-Free - Allows you to capture video without holding the record button

13. Instagram has a live video option that allows you to share content in real time. If you want to start a live video stream, simply open the camera on Instagram and then swipe to the Live setting. Then, select the prompt that says Start Live Video. Once your video has started streaming live, any of your followers that are currently on the app will be notified that you are live. These live viewers can post comments on the video using the chat feature. While the live function can be fun to use, make sure you don't go overboard by using it too often.

14. Instagram TV (IGTV) is available to watch via the Instagram app. Here, viewers can see uploaded long-form content from Instagram creators such as celebrity interviews, product reviews and tutorials, and more.

15. Your captions that complement your photos and videos are almost as important as the imagery itself. Be thoughtful in what you want to say, and seek opinions from other marketers on your team or others who are closely aligned with your brand. Captions can have up to 2,200 characters, but no matter what length your caption is unless your viewers click on More, they will only be able to see

the first few lines. So, make sure that your most important content is "above the fold."

While the above is intended to provide some helpful tips, the best way to understand the platform is to get in it and start engaging. As I've said in previous chapters, make note of what is working and what is not, and allow yourself the flexibility to evolve. The key here is to make sure you don't change in such a way that it shocks your followers out of interest.

Let's take a moment here to address shock and awe as a social marketing strategy. This journalistic approach is becoming more and more mainstream as topics that were once considered taboo are becoming more commonplace. But, understand that the entire basis of shock is intended to draw out a reaction of surprise or astonishment, which is often affiliated with anger. These negative reactions will stick with your followers and can end up doing more harm than good if not well considered. Consider these questions before trying a shock and awe tactic:

- Is the message true to your brand and your value proposition?
- Will the message create additional value?
- Will the message evoke further conversation in a positive manner that can help push an agenda?
- Will the message drive your customers to make an additional purchase?
- Will your followers want to share the message with their friends and other connections?
- How will your current and future customers react to the message?

If your answer to any one of the above questions is no or a negative response, then it is best not to pursue the shock and awe direction. This is not to say that you should stick to just vanilla content, however, as that will undoubtedly bore your followers. Rather, be thoughtful, and when something isn't working, consider minor changes that stick with your values, that allow you to better what works and what does not.

CHAPTER 9

DEVELOPING AN INFLUENCER STRATEGY

As I stated earlier in the guide, an influencer strategy is one where a marketer relies heavily (but not primarily) on others to aid in building brand awareness, building authority, and connecting with more users. These influencers help drive traffic to your business website and can result in increased conversion rates and additional followers of your brand.

Influencer marketing can drive an estimated 11x return-on-investment (ROI) over the traditional digital marketing channels, or even a social media strategy that doesn't leverage an influencer approach. In most cases, an influencer strategy is developed by identifying someone who has a strong influence on your industry or on your target audience. Your brand then forms a relationship with that influencer and the influencer agrees to expose their followers to your brand's messaging and content.

Again, using our example of an online bookseller, let's consider the impact of a celebrity and authority figure such as Oprah Winfrey, on the positive impact her support could have on your business. Now, I understand that most companies can't afford Oprah as their influencer, so I am simply using this for illustrative purposes, as I know that Oprah is an avid reader.

If your online store released a new book that is interesting to Oprah, and she agrees to promote the book over a series of posts over a determined period of time, tagging your business, this would inevitably result in additional visits to your website, and more and more users following you officially, and making purchases of the book.

Another example of celebrity influence is that of Pantene with Jada Pinkett Smith. In this instance, Jada shared Pantene's message with her Twitter audience of 1.23 million followers. Imagine the power of someone like Jada touting your brand? Again, the inevitable result is more followers of your brand, and increased conversion.

So again, this is an extreme example, and influencers like Oprah and Jada carry a price tag that most brands can't support. But, there are a variety of influencers with substantial audiences that are ready, able, and wanting to help you promote your brand, at a rate that is much more palatable for your business's budget.

How to find Instagram influencers that your business can afford

To find the right influencer for your brand, you need to go back to your target audience as you want your influencers to share the same target audience. Thinking of your target audience and your personas, who represents your brand?

- A cool and a trendy college-aged girl?
- A college-aged boy?

- A tech-savvy businessman?
- A middle-class mom of two?
- A thrifty DIYer?
- A single career-minded female looking to make her next career move?

Now that you know the type of influencer you want, consider that the right influencer has a lot of followers but those followers are engaged. Dig deep by looking at how these influencers' followers are interacting with the brand. Are they sharing comments? Videos? Are you seeing anything that goes against your brand's core values or that might offend a strong portion of your customers?

Certainly, life does happen, and even influencers with the best of intentions can find themselves in the middle of an online brawl. Know that this can happen, but that you should look for influencers that are as close as possible in their values to yours. 61% of marketers in the United States have indicated that it is challenging to find the right influencer for their brand, so understand that you are not alone here. And, many marketers share concerns about the impact if influencers to brand safety.

The common challenges of an influencer marketing strategy

So before I share some suggested platforms to help you identify your influencer(s), let's review the typical concerns that marketers have with their influencer strategies. While in no means does this below list suggest you should not proceed, it is important to enter any influencer relationship with your eyes wide open.

According to a January 2021 survey titled "Leading influencer marketing challenges according to U.S. marketers," by Mediakix, the following was discovered:

- 50% of marketers share concerns about spotting fake followers and inauthentic engagement
- 49% of marketers indicated that the social algorithm changes made content less visible
- 41% of marketers indicated that they are building an always-on strategy rather than proceeding with one-off campaigns
- 38% of marketers cited challenges with rising influencer costs
- 33% of marketers shared that it is challenging to keep up with social media trends to stay relevant
- 33% of marketers shared concerns about building a strong creative strategy
- 30% of marketers shared the need to reduce the amount of time spent on marketing campaigns
- 28% of marketers shared challenges with brand safety and brand alignment
- 18% of marketers shared concerns with federal trade commission (FTC) regulations and requirements
- 17% of marketers indicated that they are tapping into additional channels such as Twitch
- 12% of marketers indicated that they are moving influencer marketing in-house

Finding your influencers

Influencers come in all shapes and sizes, online that is. Let's start by understanding the levels of influencers so that you can determine the type that is right for you.

1. **Nano-influencers** - The first tier of influencers is referred to as nano-influencers. Marketers are more and more often giving changes to those with less followers than the traditional influencers (I'll discuss the top 25 Instagram influencers of 2021 in just a bit). These influencers have 1,000 to 5,000 followers on their account, and their followers are typically friends and others who share similar interests. In this case, it is not about followers idolizing those people, but rather, just being interested in what they have to say because they share a similar interest or passion. And a strong population of marketers (nearly half) feel that the audience relationship is the key factor in whether or not an influencer will be successful.

These influencers are considered highly approachable and are thereby very lucrative to marketers, especially those will a limited budget. These influencers come across as more trustworthy because their followers feel like their advice is genuine, and it feels like they are getting advice from a friend. Nano-influencers are also easier to contact and collaborate with as there are far fewer strings in the relationship.Usually, these influencers will promote your product for a nominal fee, or a free product from your brand.

2. **Micro-influencers** - This next tier of influencers is a group that has between 5,000 to 20,000 followers (note that some marketers view this group as having 2,000 to 50,000 followers, and in these cases, they are simply looking at fewer tiers than what I am sharing here in this Instagram Marketing Guide. These influencers are very well informed and are often experts on a particular topic. Further, they have a very engaged community of followers who are looking to the influencers to provide content that they can trust. These believe gain credibility through their authenticity because they are

everyday people sharing what they like and what they don't.

3. **Mid-tier influencers** - This middle tier has 20,000 to 100,000 followers. Their audiences are mid-sized, as the category implies, yet they generate very high engagement rates and higher engagement rates than micro-influencers.

4. **Macro-influencers** - This tier has 100,000 to 1,000,000 followers. These influencers are generally well known in their communities and have dedicated audiences that have grown over time. Their content is very high in quality and is focused on something that the macro-influencer is passionate for. Marketers often like working with macro-influencers as they are far more affordable than the next tier, and their content is rarely impacted by algorithms that limit who feeds get to. As such, these influencers have very good reach which results in very good engagement. In many cases, macro-influencers product their content using professional equipment, and these professionals have taken time to hone their craft and their tone of voice.

5. **Mega-influencers** - These influencers are just that, mega, with an impressive following of over 1,000,000. As such, these people are the upper echelon in the influencer community, but also have the highest fees (Kylie Jenner charges $1,000,000 per sponsored social media post). The benefit is that mega-influencers have a variety of interests with diverse audiences, so they reach a lot of people, quite often, and as such, they often work with big brands with big marketing budgets.

So who are the big mega influencers? Below let's take a look at the top 25 influencers on Instagram for 2021.

So, let's now focus on how to find those influencers that are within your budget, now that you understand the various influencer tiers and the benefits of each.

There are a variety of platforms available to help you discover and engage with influencers that can positively help your brand. Key platforms include (but are not limited to) Upfluence, Buzzsumo, and HypeAuditor.

Each of these platforms comes with its own pros and cons, so be sure to review the platforms available and determine the one best for you, and for your budget. Also, as you grow awareness of your brand through Instagram, you may find influencers organically through followers who tend to comment on or share your content frequently. In these cases, and if they have a strong follower base (or a desire to grow it), consider sending these folks a direct message to start a conversation and to explore if they would want to become an influencer for you. Often these *pre-nano-influencers* can be enticed to become more of an informal influencer for you if you offer them a simple gesture of some kind, such as sending them a free product, gift card, or nominal one-time compensation.

CHAPTER 10

BEST TIME TO POST YOUR CONTENT

While there isn't an exact science on when to post your content, studies have been done to show when posts are more likely to generate interest and engagement. Later.com, an marketing platform for Instagram, conducted an analysis of 12,000,000 Instagram posts and found that the best time of day to post is between 9AM to 11AM ET. But even though that was the best time identified by this particular survey, it might not be the right time for your business. But before I go into how to identify the best time for you, let's take a look at the best times identified globally, by day of week.

In most cases, posting between 9AM to 6PM (during your time zone), during the work week, will generate the best engagement. This is because people tend to visit social sites during the workday vs. after work or on with the weekends when they are more likely engaged in family and fun activities. However, many people check their phones immediately upon waking in the morning, which provides a great idea to plant some content in their minds before they go about their day.

In most cases, engagement on Mondays is relatively low as people are returning to work after a weekend off. People tend to check their social media accounts during their lunch breaks, and again during the late afternoon when energy levels start to fade after a long day at work. On the weekends, Saturday mornings tend to be active as parents check in while their kids are off at various activities, and Sundays often have a bit more activity as Sundays tend to be the more relaxed of the two weekend days.

- Sunday: 10AM to 2PM
- Monday: 11AM to 5PM
- Tuesday: 5AM, 9AM to 6PM
- Wednesday: 5AM,11AM to 3PM
- Thursday: 5AM, 11AM, 3PM - 4PM
- Friday: 5AM, 9AM - 4PM
- Saturday: 11AM

Now that you understand the most popular times for people to consider engagement, let's take a look at the best days of the week to post. Again, this may be different for your business, but this is a good place to start. In order of best to worst, the best days of week are listed below:

1. Wednesday
2. Thursday
3. Tuesday
4. Friday
5. Saturday
6. Sunday
7. Monday

As you have reviewed the above information, a natural follow-on question is regarding time zones. In this case, it is important to understand the time zone that is most prevalent for your target audience. So, if your primary audience is on the east coast, then, you should use the eastern time zone and apply it to the directional guidance provided above.

If your followers tend to be geographically dispersed, you may want to create a time zone map that shows the various locations of your audience, and then look for windows of potential overlap so that some of your posts can be multi-purpose, serving more than one time zone at once. If this sounds complicated, don't fret, as Instagram has built-in tools that can make this a bit easier.

With insight into when most users are engaging in the Instagram platform, the next step is to explore if it is different for your target audience. Within your business account, you will have the ability to use Instagram Insights to analyze the demographics of your followers, as well as their engagement and level of activity. This provides you with information that you can use to develop your content calendar and posting schedule.

Your Instagram Insights data is accessible to you through your account page on the Instagram app. Tap n the bar graph icon at the top of the screen, and you'll see helpful information about post and story performance. You'll also be able to get key data points about impressions, comments, shares, and how you are gaining (or losing) followers.

Take some time to check out this feature on your app, and be sure to watch the data regularly going forward. As your audience begins to grow, you will notice that their most active times may shift as well, and this will provide you with the insight you need to tailor your content to align with what will resonate with them post.

CONCLUSION

If you've made it this far in the guided, chances are your brain is full to the brim with new knowledge and key ideas, and you are ready to put everything you have learned into action.

As I stated at the beginning of this guide, social media marketing, and Instagram marketing in particular, is a must for your company. Let's reiterate the significance here:

1. Your customers are on social media
2. Social media marketing helps grow brand awareness and authority
3. Social media marketing will help you improve brand loyalty
4. Social media marketing grows inbound traffic (web visits *and* store/location visits)
5. Social media marketing allows you to target and retarget your customers and future customers
6. Social media marketing is much more cost-effective than more traditional channels
7. Social media marketing can help you improve your rankings with various search engines
8. Your competition is on social media

9. Social media marketing is proven to lead to increased conversation rates
10. Consumers like to see recommendations that are provided to them on social media
11. Social media marketing will help you grow your customer base

In this guide, my goal was to inform you, and ensure you were better equipped to develop an Instagram marketing strategy for your business. And I hope that I have achieved just that by introducing you to the basics of Instagram, helping you to identify goals and objectives and set up your business profile, by helping you determine your niche, by providing you the tips and tricks to develop high-quality content, by helping you understand how to use hashtags and get new users, by educating you on how to pursue and leverage influencers, and by showing you the best time of day and the best day of week to engage your followers.

If all of the above didn't stick, I hope that you'll read the book again, but also that you will in the least, take away a new respect and knowledge about the power of marketing on Instagram. If you have decided for whatever reason that now is not the right time for you to start, I hope that you now have the tools you need, so that you can jumpstart the process when you determine you *are* ready.

Social Media Marketing Guide 2021

Gain Customers through Facebook, YouTube, and Twitter

INTRODUCTION TO SOCIAL MEDIA MARKETING

It is amazing to reflect on where the internet has taken us. As we approach the 28-year anniversary of the availability of the world wide web to the public, it really is impressive where we are today and how social media has become a primary source of news, information, and communication.

With LinkedIn's release in 2003, Facebook in 2004, YouTube in 2005, Twitter in 2006, and Pinterest and Instagram in 2010, marketers have been faced with an entirely different set of challenges, and opportunities in reaching their audiences. And with 2 billion users on social platforms combined, it is no wonder that marketers have made social media marketing a priority.

Social media marketing, in the broadest sense, is the process of drumming up attention for your business, through a social media site. This list below provides a high-level overview of the various social media sites available today, and the estimated monthly active users.

- Facebook = 2.23 billion monthly active users
- Instagram = 1 billion monthly active users
- LinkedIn = 260 million monthly active users
- Pinterest = 250 million monthly active users
- Snapchat = 300+ million monthly active users

- Twitter = 326 million monthly active users

Determining the correct social media site or sites to engage in with your customers and prospective customers is often a matter of personal or business preference. And, it is often based on the number of users that your business can get in front of. With 59% of people accessing social media at least one time (or more) each day, these sites provide an excellent and convenient way to grow brand awareness for your business.

Why is social media marketing a must for your company?

1. It is highly likely that your customers are on social media
2. With the prevalence of and preference for social media as a news and information outlet, your customers very likely want to be engaged in one of these sites
3. Social media marketing helps grow brand awareness and authority
4. Social media marketing can help you improve brand loyalty
5. Social media marketing grows inbound traffic (web visits and store/location visits)
6. Social media marketing allows you to target and retarget your customers and future customers but allows you to control frequency to keep interested without creating annoyance
7. Social media marketing is much more cost-effective than many of the more traditional channels
8. Social media marketing can help you improve your rankings with various search engines
9. Your competition is definitely on social media

10. Social media marketing is proven to lead to increased conversation rates

11. Consumers like to see (and follow) recommendations that are provided to them on social media

12. Social media marketing can help you grow your customer base

13. Social media sites often provide insight capabilities for businesses so that they can learn more about their customers

When your business engages with social media and pays attention to what your customers and potential customers are doing and saying, you gain insight into what they care about. This provides you with the ability to solve your customer's challenges and concerns, as well as understand what they want to see so that you can tailor your content accordingly. These actions on the part of your business will have an inevitable positive result on customer service and your customers' perceptions of you.

In this guide, we'll explore the history of each platform, and how to develop and implement a successful marketing program on each.

Dispelling the misconceptions about social media marketing

Even though social media marketing has become a mainstay for all marketers, there still remain some misconceptions, which I will dispel here.

1. All social media platforms are the same - This is absolutely not the case as each social media platform was created for a particular purpose.

2. Marketers need a presence on all social media channels - While I don't suggest putting all of your eggs in one basket and you will learn in this guide

about the benefits of integration with Facebook, it is not necessary for you to be on all channels, especially if you do not have the resources to manage content consistently.

3. Social media is for younger people - While it is true that use varies by age, it is also true that all age groups have a representation on social media.88% of 18-29-year-olds use social media, as does 78% of Americans age 30-49, 64% of Americans age 50-64, and 37% of Americans age 65+.

4. Social media doesn't have a role in all industries - This couldn't be further from the truth. Social media provides a mechanism for any industry to gain brand awareness, whether selling a product or service or just to put thought leadership on your industry and relevant learnings out into the market.

5. Social media is free - It is true that you can set up a social media account at no cost. However, social media advertising, content development, imagery production, etc. can all come at a cost, especially when looking to generate content of high-quality.

6. Social media can't be measured - At this point, most social media channels have begun offering insight tools that can aid in the measurement of clicks, read-through, and a variety of other key performance indicators (KPIs).

7. It's all about the hashtags - I'll spend time reviewing the hashtag strategy later in this guide. And hashtags are important. However, it is possible to overdo it, so remember that the hashtag strategy is all about relevance, connection, organization, and balance.

8. Social media is time-consuming - Indeed it can be. But, it is also the cheapest form of advertising available. You can gain exposure to over 1,000

people, for less than the cost of a cup of your favorite Starbucks beverage.

9. Negative comments are bad for your business - Yes, negative word of mouth can have unfortunate ramifications, but research shows that companies that engage with their unsatisfied (and satisfied) customers gain more loyalty and repeat transactions than those that do not.

10. Your competition will always be a step ahead of you - If you don't have a social media presence and they do, yes, you are behind. But by reading this guide and taking our suggestions and implementing them in your business, you will have the opportunity to not only catch up but also hopefully outshine.

11. It doesn't matter how often I post as long as I am sure to post sometimes - You'll learn in this guide that frequency is important, but so too is consistency. Your customers will be looking for predictability, and you can also leverage time of day and day of week suggestions to ensure you are maximizing your brand exposure.

12. Social media marketing is a fad that will pass by soon - Word of mouth marketing has played a role for decades, and since social media presents a forum for users to share their opinions, it is highly unlikely that it will go away anytime soon.

13. I can stick to traditional marketing and be just as successful - As social media provides the best mechanism today to build brand awareness and provides some of the best reach available, it would be very unfortunate for any marketer to pass this opportunity by.

Quite simply, social media marketing is drastically changing the game for businesses of all sizes. But, it is critical to have realistic marketing goals, as well as returns on investment

(ROI). While ROI will vary among different businesses, here are five examples of ROI that can be generated through effective social media marketing:

- An increase in user engagement - measured through user comments, likes, and shares
- A more thorough understanding of your followers by actively communicating with them - we'll be talking about social listening and response in a follow-on chapter
- An ability to reach new customers through the networks of your followers
- An ability to differentiate your business from that of your competition
- An ability to increase sales and grow revenue for your business

In this book, I will provide you with the steps you need to start using these channels successfully in your business. Let's dive into:

- Why social media marketing is a must for your business
- The benefits of niche marketing
- Creating goals for effective social media campaigns
- Facebook marketing
- YouTube marketing
- Twitter marketing
- The best time of day and day of the week to post social media content
- The importance of an influencer strategy
- Developing an influencer strategy

After reading this guide, I promise that you will be more informed and better equipped to develop a social marketing strategy on Facebook, YouTube, and Twitter for your business. If you don't have a presence on these social sites yet, the time to start is right now. Better yet, this guide has been designed to provide just the right level of detail to get you started.

So what are you waiting for? Read on and start improving your customer engagement today.

CHAPTER 1

THE RISE OF SOCIAL MEDIA IN NICHE MARKETING

You may be wondering why I am talking about niche so early in this guide. And quite simply, that is because in many ways, niche marketing was meant for social media, and social media was meant for niche marketing.

With traditional media, such as television ads and billboards, you are really taking a spray and pray approach. If you're not familiar with the spray and pray term, think of this hunting scenario of leveraging a shotgun to hit your target, instead of a sniper rifle. The shotgun sprays its ammunition all over, and if the shooter gets lucky, it might hit its target. But a sniper zooms in and hits the target directly. In no way does this mean I am taking an opinion about hunting, rather, this description is the best way to understand the spray and pray concept.

With social media, users are most likely to spend time on platforms and sites that align to their interests, and they will follow other users that align with their interests as well. So, this makes customers much easier to find than ever before.

But, remember that social media is available to anyone and everyone, so that means your competition can reach your customers this way too. Your goal is to capture those customers before they do.

If you have identified your niche already, congratulations. You are ready to move on to the next chapter. If not, let's take some time to ensure you understand the difference between a niche and your target market or audience. A niche defines the service or products that you specialize in, and want to advertise to your potential buyers. Your target market is those potential buyers that are hopefully interested in your niche.

Understanding your target market is important because you need to understand where to find them so that you can develop your marketing strategy, and so that your market will understand that your offerings are dedicated to them and their interests. Further, your target market will already have networks of communication in place, as it is a market, and not just an individual. This means that those within your market are likely interacting with one another and with many of the same modes of communication available to them such as magazines, social forums, etc.

The niche is then your area of specialization that you want to be known for. Often, this means you are leveraging some form of differentiation that sets you apart from other service providers or manufacturers or businesses that offer something similar to your product or service.

Understanding how you are different from other providers is critical to defining your niche. Generally, your differentiator must be true and important to your potential customers. Further, you need to be able to prove it. You can't just say that you are different because your customers will expect you to be able to tell them how you are different.

If you're not sure of your niche, consider these questions below to narrow it down.

1. Write down your businesses interests and passions. How and why did your company get its start?
2. What are the business problems for others that you are trying to solve? What conversations have you had with your target market to date, and what have they told you?
3. Who is your competition? How long have they been in business and how did they get their start? What does their marketing content look like? Do they have a presence on social media platforms? How many followers do they have and what do those followers, as a general group, look like?
4. Is your perceived niche profitable? If people don't actually want to solve their business problem, then you won't be able to generate revenue. And if your target market is incredibly small, and your product or services are a one-time need, then it may be difficult to make money long term. Your goal here is to ensure that your niche will be profitable for years to come.
5. Have you tested your idea, live in the market? This is different than the initial focus group testing that you need during the product development phase. Rather, this is about testing your finished product by setting up your company website and driving traffic to your site with paid advertising tactics. If people aren't coming to your site, what type of A/B testing have you done to play with various subject lines, offers, etc. to see what best resonates?

If you weren't able to answer the above questions, chances are that you really don't have a niche. If that is the case, I implore you to keep searching. If you want your business to be able to scale, you really need a niche.

The Benefits of Niche Marketing

When niche marketing is done correctly, it can have many benefits.

- Improved customer relationships - While you need to right-size your niche (if your niche is too small, you might not be in business for very long), there are benefits to a smaller customer base. This allows you to focus on quality interactions that will win them over.
- Reduced competition - If you took the time to thoroughly answered the questions I asked earlier in this chapter, you understand who your competition is, and what they are focusing on. Further, you know how you are different. The key now is to stay different, but not become complacent. You should have your eye on the market at all times so that you can watch for changes in consumer perceptions and needs. If the market starts to change, you need to change with it (and hopefully just far enough ahead of it that your customers will stay with you).
- Enhanced visibility - Businesses that are unique get more attention from media outlets. This could mean an article in the newspaper (and if you get mentioned in the newspaper, that article will be online, and that can become social media gold), or a seat on a morning talk show that targets your ideal customer set. While you need to focus on getting in front of the right people, don't sweat it if you get in front of a few others that don't fit within your niche. If they like what they hear, they might talk about you to someone who is. And that is a perfect lead-in to our next point.
- Word of mouth advertising - People in your niche are likely talking to other people in your niche, and if they like what they hear, they'll talk about you. But even people that might not be in your niche could

> pick up on something about your business and pass it on. So again, this is about quality messaging. If you have to pick quality over quantity, quality should win, every time.

Judge Graham, a Texas-based entrepreneur, and investor who was quoted in a September 2018 Forbes article, stated that owning your niche immediately gives you a leg-up on other businesses in the space. He also stated, "Forty-percent of startups fail, mostly because they ignore the opportunity to capitalize on a niche and don't actually provide a solution to a problem. That means almost half of all startup ideas are worthless. That's a lot of wasted time, money, and effort. If you're only a generalist, unfortunately, you might as well just quit then and there."

CHAPTER 2

CREATING GOALS FOR EFFECTIVE SOCIAL MEDIA MARKETING

Before you try to develop any type of social media marketing strategy, you need to take the time to set some goals. Without goals, it's quite difficult, if not impossible, to determine how well your social media strategy is performing. Clear and actionable goals will propel your strategy forward, and will also serve as clear metrics when it comes to measuring and reporting on your progress and campaign performance.

Here is a list of some of the most common goals that are used to measure the success of a social media marketing strategy:

- Drive traffic to your website
- Sell a product
- Advertise a service
- Increase sales
- Generate more inbound leads

- Communicate with customers
- Increase brand awareness
- Establish online authority as a thought leader in the industry

Setting SMART social media marketing goals

SMART goal setting brings structure and measurement ability to your goals and objectives. Instead of vague goals that are often subjective in nature and hard to put numbers behind, SMART goal setting creates clarity around what is expected for a certain objective, with clear milestones and an estimation of the goal's attainability. Every goal or objective can be developed using the SMART concept, and will provide a sense of reality to you, your marketing team, and your leadership team.

For marketers SMART goal setting is viewed as one of the most efficient and practical tools used for specifying and achieving goals. If you aren't familiar with the concept of a SMART goal, please review the following explanations.

- Specific — The more specific you can be with the goal, the easier it will be for you and your team to understand what you are trying to achieve.
- Measurable — This is pretty self-explanatory - how will you measure your success?
- Attainable — Is your goal attainable?
- Relevant — A goal that is relevant is aligned closely to your business objectives. Consider if this goal supports your business's objectives, vision, or values. If it doesn't, then it is the wrong goal.
- Timebound — Give your goal a deadline. By when do you want to have achieved this goal?

Defining Your SMART Goals

Ensure that your goals are documented in such a way that your entire marketing organization, as well as relevant business leaders, have access to your goals. Consider setting up your dashboard in a Google doc or sheet, or leverage a dashboard capability within your marketing technology stack. Whatever you do, make sure you document the following:

- The date the goal was set (today's date if you are documenting your goals right now)
- Date by which you plan to achieve your goal
- Your goal in one sentence
    - Specific: What exactly will you accomplish?
    - Measurable: How will you and your team know when you have reached your goal?
    - Attainable: Is attaining this goal realistic with effort and commitment? Do you have the resources to achieve this goal? If not, how will you get them?
    - Relevant: Why is this goal important to you? Hone in on why it matters.
    - Time-bound: When will you achieve this goal?
- The benefits of achieving your goal

Let's write a goal for the marketing team for our cupcake shop. In this case, our favorite bakers have decided to enhance the blog strategy that they rolled out the previous year. So, their goal will focus on blog traffic. In their goal document, they have written the following:

- Specific: We will boost our blog's traffic by increasing our weekly publishing frequency from 5 to 8 times a week. Our freelance bloggers can increase their weekly workload from writing 2 posts to 3 posts, and our freelance editor will increase her workload from writing 1 post a week to 2 posts a week.

- Measureable: An 8% increase is our goal.
- Attainable: Our blog traffic increased by 5% last month after we increased our weekly publishing frequency from 3 to 5 times per week.
- Relevant: By increasing blog traffic, we'll boost brand awareness and generate more leads, giving sales more opportunities to close.
- Timebound: End of this month

The SMART goal, in sentence form, becomes: At the end of this month, our bakery blog will see an 8% lift in traffic because we will increase our weekly publishing frequency from 5 posts per week to 8 posts per week.

Create Your SMART Goal Measurement Plan

Now that your goal is clearly documented, you need to outline your plan to measure progress towards the goal. This is about accountability, so make sure that your measurement plan is publicly available to those who need to know. The more public your goal is in your organization, the more will you hold yourself and your team accountable.

- Network of Support & Accountability. When working towards achieving a goal, it is helpful to take a partner (or two) whom you agree to check in with on a regular basis. Keeping others informed on your progress can be a useful external motivator. This person might be your boss, or even the Chief Marketing Officer (CMO).
- Frequency of updates on progress. Will you share updates weekly, bi-weekly, monthly? This may be dependent on your business's approach to performance reporting. If your leadership team gets together monthly to review results, then you will want to build a monthly reporting rhythm that

allows you to bring an updated dashboard to the meeting so that results can be shared.

- Agreed upon method of communication. Will you share updates face-to-face in a meeting, over the phone, via an internal messaging system, via company email, or in some other fashion? Where will the results be kept for future reference?

Another helpful step in the goal process is to develop an action plan that clearly outlines who is responsible for what, and by when. As items are completed, they can either be crossed off the list, or the completion date can be added in another column (if you are using a spreadsheet type of tracking document).

CHAPTER 3

THE BEGINNING OF FACEBOOK

Facebook was founded in 2004 by Mark Zuckerberg, Eduardo Saverin, Dustin Moskovitz, and Chris Hughes. These four men were students at Harvard University, and the original platform name was Facemash. The initial purpose was so that fellow students at Harvard could judge how attractive their classmates were. However, Zuckerberg violated university policy in acquiring resources for the service, and it was shut down in a matter of days. Despite its short lifespan, Facemash acquired 450 people who voted 22,000 times.

The popularity of Facemash drove Zuckerberg to later the domain TheFacebook in early 2004. The URL http://www.thefacebook.com was created as a new social network, in partnership with

Saverin, Moskovitz, and Hughes. The initial platform was limited to students at Harvard, who could sign up for the service and then post their photographs, and a limited amount of information about their personal lives. They were able to post class schedules, co-curricular clubs that they participated in, etc. As time went on, the popularity of the platform grew, and before long, students from Yale and Stanford were able to join.

However, despite the initial success, Zuckerberg and his co-founders were accused just six days after the site launched that they had stolen the idea from Cameron and Tyler Winklevoss and Divya Narendra. According to the Winklevoss brothers and Narendra, they had asked Zuckerberg for his help in creating a social network for their classmates, which would be named HarvardConnection.

According to the Winklevoss twins and Narendra, they had approached Zuckerberg asking for his assistance in creating a social network for Harvard students called "HarvardConnection." A lawsuit was filed against Zuckerberg, and the three claimants received 1.2 million shares in the company each, as part of a settlement in 2008. This legal claim was actually glamourized in the 2010 film titled The Social Network, which shows Zuckerberg, the Winklevoss brothers, and Narenda discussing the idea.

More than 250,000 students from 34 schools had signed up for TheFacebook by June 2004, and shortly thereafter, MasterCard started paying for advertising exposure on the site. In September 2004, the site added a new feature called "the wall" which allowed members to post information on their personal page, aka their "wall," and this practice took off and would go on to become a key element in social media.

By the time 2004 had come to a close, TheFacebook had over one million users but was still lagging behind MySpace, which had over five million. But Zuckerberg and team continued to innovate, and in 2005, the tagging feature became available, which allowed users to tag themselves, and others, in images on the site. There was no limit to the number of photos that someone could upload to their page, and it wasn't long before high-school students and students at colleges and universities outside of the United States were able to sign-up.

By the end of 2005, TheFacebook had six million monthly active users and had surpassed the success of MySpace. In 2006, the site was opened to anyone age 13 or over. With this exponential growth and interest from consumers all over the world, it created a new advertising opportunity for advertisers, that had never been considered before. Also in 2005, TheFacebook became Facebook, which is the name we all know for the platform today.

By 2012, Facebook had become the largest social network in the world, with more than one billion users. Further, 50% of those users were visiting the site every day.

Facebook Becomes a Platform for Marketers

Before we get into the details of how to build your Facebook marketing strategy, it is important to understand the size of the prize.

- As of the third quarter of 2018, there were 2.375 billion active users per month
- Over 1bn of those are mobile-only users
- There are 1.49 billion daily active users
- 47% of Facebook users only access the platform through mobile
- Facebook adds 500,000 new users every day; six new profiles every second
- 68% of US adults use Facebook - 51% of them use it several times a day
- 26.3% of the worldwide online population use Facebook
- Users spend an average of 20 minutes per day on the site
- There are over 60 million active business pages
- Facebook claimed 19% of the $70 billion spent on mobile advertising worldwide in 2015

- 78% of Facebook advertising revenue comes from mobile ads
- 49% of users like a Facebook page to support a brand they like
- 40% of users don't like any brand pages – meaning paid adverts are the only way to reach them

These statistics should make it quite clear as to why a presence, and an active presence on Facebook, is important for your business. So, it's time to get started.

How to Set Up a Business Account on Facebook

Now that you have seen the statistics, you understand that it is easier than ever for your target audience to find you, and interact with you, online. And setting up a business account is easy. Follow these steps:

1. Sign Up - Navigate to https://www.facebook.com/business and click Create a Page, which should be located towards the center of your screen. You will need to select whether or not you are a Business or Brand or a Community of Public Figure. As an example in this chapter, I'll say we are an Organic Cupcake Shop. So, this means we are a business, and we need to click on Get Started for the applicable box. Now, you will be asked for a few more details such as the name of your business, your business address, and your page category. For the page category, simply start typing in the type of business you have, and a variety of options will pop up. In this case, if we start to type cupcake, we get options for Cupcake Shop and for Bakery. At this point, take a moment to select the category that makes sense for your business, and then select Continue.
2. Add your profile photo and cover photo. Make sure to select photos that best represent your business.

A wise choice is your logo for your profile, as this will help with brand recognition and recall. Then, for your cover photo, an image of your store or primary product (such as a cupcake) will work well.

3. When prompted to set up your Facebook URL, do not simply accept the dynamic URL that Facebook suggests. On Facebook, you can personalize your URL and unify it with your brand name, which makes it unique and easy for you and your customers to remember. When you match your Facebook URL with the page's title, you will strengthen your brand recognition. And, personalization will improve the ability for customers to find you on Facebook.

4. Create a call to action. This directs your visits to do something, such as visit your website, call your store, etc. It is highly recommended that you enable this feature.

5. Your account is now set-up and it is ready to take action. Read on for what to do next.

6. Get Company Employees to Like your Company Business Page

Now that your account is live on Facebook, you can start engaging with customers. But in order to engage with customers, you need to get them first. The best way to start is to get your employees tied to the account, by asking them to like the page, and then to share it with their networks. This might feel a bit like cheating, but it really is a great way to help you get started. That said, it is important that when you ask company employees to like the page, that you also share your company's rules around social media engagement. If your company does not yet have a social media policy, it is important to work with your human resources and legal partners to get one in place, and to ensure it is properly communicated to all company employees.

There are many benefits to a social media policy (note that this social media policy applies to all social platforms, not just Facebook).

- Protects you from security risks and keeps you out of legal trouble
- Empowers employees to be ambassadors of your company
- Provides employees with the guidelines on what they can communicate and what they can't on social channels
- Provides clarification on the company's values and culture for employees as well as for customers and the public
- Enables consistency across all social platforms
- Sets expectations for brand new employees joining the organization to ensure proper behaviors and expectations are articulated up front
- Enables the company to assign responsibility for content control and approvals.
- Improve productivity and reduce lost time spent dealing with unauthorized usage of social media, including dealing with the consequences of conflict related to social media use.
- Reduce risk and legal exposure for the business.

So, what should you include in your social media policy? In the least, be sure to include the following:

- The rules - This is about proper employee conduct, such as representing the company in a positive manner, no swearing, no inappropriate photos, etc. The rules should also include:

- How to talk about your company and products
- Etiquette and engagement: How you want employees to respond to mentions of your brand (positive and negative) - in most cases, this will be handled by a designated member of the marketing team, and should not be a free-for-all for any employee to respond to comments made on the platform
- Clarity on company information that may not be shared on social media
- Clear consequences for employees and managers on the abuse of social media
- How and when employees can use social media while at work (if at all)

- Roles and responsibilities tied to the following tasks:
    - Message approval - who is responsible for deciding what the company posts on various social media platforms.
    - Crisis response - If a national emergency has happened, if your company has been involved in a lawsuit, etc., this section should outline who manages those communications and what, if anything, is said on social media. This person is not always a marketing person.
    - Social media monitoring/ listening and response - This is the practice of watching for posts from customers, and ensuring that those comments, both positive and negative, are responded to in a timely manner. In most cases, it is suggested that customer comments are responded to within 24 hours or less. Remember, responding to a negative comment is critical - and it could be the difference

between whether or not that customer will give your business another chance. And acknowledging positive comments is important too. Customers want to know that their comments have been seen.

- Legal & security risks - This should outline any potential legal ramifications that an employee could be subject to for misuse of company social media platforms.

Now that employees know the rules for social media engagement as it relates to your company, and have liked the business page, it is time to start getting those customers to like your page too.

How to Engage Customers on Facebook

Here are 24 suggestions to help you grow your Facebook company page, attract more likes, and capture the attention and following of your target market.

1. Use images that represent or speak to your business
2. Post content that meets your customer's needs and addresses their pain points
3. Use social plug-ins on your website and blogs so that visitors can easily share your content
4. If your company has a customer email strategy, make sure that every email ends with a call to action that includes a link back to your website. And even better, ensure that at the bottom of your emails, you include links to your social channels.
5. In those emails, periodically invite customers to follow you on your social channels by providing them with easy links for access. Do this especially when you first launch your channels, but then periodically (or at the bottom of every email) to remind customers on where to find you.

6. Ensure you have a content curation strategy that aligns to your content development strategy. This means that you should be regularly liking content from others that aligns with your core messages and that you share that content on occasion too. This doesn't mean you should be sharing your customer's content. But, for example, our Cupcake Shop might want to share a post from TLC's The Next Great Baker, as it aligns with their company (a bakery). This is a great way to keep your customers interested, but not make it all about you. Make sure that this content curation strategy is done from the company social pages, and not from your personal pages (though that is a great secondary strategy).

7. Cross-promote your messages across sites. Twitter followers or Instagram connections might find relevant content or discussions happening on your Facebook page, and that gives you more bang for your buck.

8. Engage your customers with contests such as photo contests. The contest doesn't necessarily have to have a prize associated with it either. For example, Delta Airlines encourages their loyal SkyMiles members to post photos to Delta's social media sites, using hashtags such as #SkyMilesLife and/or #DeltaMedallionLife. I'll talk more about hashtags later, but this strategy is a great way to create a sense of community amongst your customers. For our cupcake shop, a great contest could be to have customers post photos of cupcakes made at home.

9. Don't overdo your promotional content. Make 80% of your content informational and informative and the other 20% promotional. For example, our cupcake shop could release one blog post a week with different cupcake recipes, our even a blog on the top appliances for bakers. Of course, the goal is

to get people to come into the shop to buy cupcakes, keeping them interested in baking-related content will actually help keep your customers coming in.

10. Encourage employees to create a link to your company Facebook page from their personal Facebook page. An easy way to do this is in their About section; they can simply do a search for your company and list that as their employer.

11. The shorter the post, the better your engagement. When sharing content on Facebook, keep the intro short and to the point. Of course, if sharing a link to an interesting article or to your company blog, you should tell your audience why you are sharing the link, but keep it brief.

12. Encourage your followers to tag themselves when they share photos on your site. And, be sure to thank them by responding to their post.

13. Videos are key in social media. I'll have a separate chapter in our YouTube section about the power of video, and you should be sure to check that out. But in the meantime, know that video plays a critical role on Facebook, and you can load your video right on your Facebook page (this is called native video), and you can then take the source code and share it on your website or other social channels.

14. Leverage Facebook to share coupon or discount codes that can only be found on your Facebook page. Of course, it is possible that your code will get shared to non-Facebook followers, but don't worry about that, because it might mean your code just got shared with a new-to-you customer.

15. I talk about this in Instagram Marketing Guide 2021, but play up the holidays... all of them. This isn't just about your typical holidays such as Christmas, or Easter, or Mother's Day, or Father's Day. Think

about those unique holidays such as National Siblings Day... capture a great photo of one of your employees doing something special with their sibling that day and turn that into content for Facebook (and for all of your social channels). If your company practices green strategies, be sure to capture those actions on film and share them on Earth Day. Look for those unique opportunities to participate in the stories that captivate others. This is about getting personal, and giving your customers a look at who you are, behind the scenes too.

16. Include "follow me on Facebook" messages and links (for Facebook as well as your other social channels) on all forms of media, including company business cards, magazine advertisements, brochures, letterhead, and even on sales presentation decks.

17. If your company has a physical location, such as in the case with our cupcake shop, add signage, even if just on a placard on the front receptionist desk, that includes a call to action to follow your company on social media. For small retailers and service shops like the cupcake shop, a nail salon, a hair stylist, etc., add a message that indicates that if they leave you a positive review on social media, that you will reward them with a discount the next time they come make a purchase at your establishment.

18. Optimize your site and remember the value of SEO (search engine optimization). Incorporate keywords throughout your Facebook business page. Place your targeted keywords in the most important sections of your page, such as in the URL, page title, and "About us" section. The name of your page corresponds with the title tag and your short description works as the meta description (a snippet of up to about 155 characters – a tag in

HTML – which summarizes your page's content) tag. But, don't overuse keywords either. Come up with the most important key words (five to seven) and then only use them when appropriate and within the proper context. Finally, understand that the first 18 characters of your Facebook posts become the meta title and meta description in search engine results pages (SERPs).

19. Consider creating a Facebook group, which will enable your company to interact with your customers. A Facebook group is a place for communication amongst a small group of people so that they can express their opinions and engage in conversation. The group function is an added value for your customers and in providing a group, it gives them the sense of exclusivity, making them feel special to be so important to your company.

20. Don't be afraid to tag other pages as part of your post strategy. Your posts will then appear on their wall, and can spark additional interest and conversation.

21. Remember the importance of a niche, and leave relevant comments on other blogs in your niche, even if they are from your competition (though be fair and appropriate). Link to your company Facebook page when asked for a URL, whenever possible (though this will not be appropriate when commenting on a competitor's post).

22. When you post on the walls of your customers or other company's be sure to add an @ tag for your company page.

23. Add a "Like us on Facebook:" message and link to your company's website thank you page. Customers will often engage shortly after making a purchase.

24. Post regularly and predictably, not just when you come to think of it. Businesses that post sporadically make it look like they are not investing in their customers regularly. Further, customers will look for a pattern over time, and will be expecting great and enriching content.

25. Taking it to the next level - Facebook advertising

Now that your Facebook account has set-up, and you've had the opportunity to explore different ways to promote content, it is time to understand how to advertise on Facebook. Facebook is presently one of the top online advertising channels. In fact, over 50% of total advertising spend in the United States, occurs on Facebook. The rationale for this is quite simple; almost 80% American consumers have indicated that they have made a product purchase because of Facebook.

The process to set-up a Facebook campaign is quite simple. But, before we get into detail, let's review the benefits of Facebook advertising.

- Internet users spend an average of 2 hours and 22 minutes per day on social networking platforms, and messaging platforms.
- Facebook had 2.38 billion monthly active users, as of early 2021.
- Facebook has been reducing the visibility of business pages in people's news feeds, frustrating business owners everywhere. And, of course, this is a strategy to help Facebook make money. Since most participation on Facebook is free, then it makes sense that in order to get in front of your fans, you are going to have to advertise.
- Facebook ads can amplify the reach of your content as when influencers (more on influencers in a later chapter) share your ads, your content becomes

exposed to a larger audience. This can help engagement to snowball.

- Facebook ads can be targeted to users based on demographics, geography, age, gender, interests, behaviors, and their connections.
- The click to call function can be extremely beneficial, and this option is only available as part of Facebook's advertising. When a customer clicks to call your business, you get the opportunity to engage directly. This is far more valuable than a visit to your website, which may or may not lead to a future conversation.

So, how exactly do you set up an ad on Facebook? Thankfully, Facebook has made it exceptionally easy to build an ad. You can set up your ad in a variety of formats as well, which can help to reach more customers.

- Video - According to Facebook, 78% of all mobile data will be video by 2021. Shorter videos have higher completion rates, but longer videos allow you share more information. Later in this guide, we will explore the use of video across the sales funnel. Be sure to reference that section to better understand the ideal length for your video content.
- Image - Using a photo ad on Facebook is a great way to increase awareness of who you are and what you do. Your customers will be better able to remember your content, if it is complemented by an engaging image.
- Collection - Facebook Collections is an ad format that lets users move through the purchase cycle in a smooth and immersive way. Each collection ad features a primary video or image that is accompanied by four smaller images, in a grid-like layout. When a customer taps on your collection ad to browse, they are taken to a fast-loading visual

experience that allows them to see your various products.

- Carousel - This ad format is available for Facebook, Instagram, Messenger and Audience Network. It allows you to showcase ten images or videos within a single ad, and each ad will have its own link. With more creative space within an ad, you can highlight different products, showcase specific details about one product, service or promotion, or tell a story about your brand.
- Slideshow - You can use motion, text, and sound tell your brand story on any connection speed. Slideshows are created within the Facebook Ads Manager and run as video ads.
- Instant experience - This is an experience that opens after a user interacts with your ad on a mobile device, and it shows as fullscreen.
- Lead generation ads - Your customers and prospective customers want to hear from your brand, but completing even the simplest of website forms can be difficult on a mobile device. Lead generation ads makes the lead generation process easy, as customers can simply tap your ad and a form pops up — it's already pre-populated with their Facebook contact information and ready to be sent directly to you, as a marketing qualified lead (MQL).
- Offers - A discount or promotion is a great way to get the attention of your customers and to encourage them to take action. With Facebook offer ads, marketers can create and extend discounts and timely promotions to those you want to reach, thus encouraging them to shop.
- Post engagement - These ads help you share information about your business with users. You

can use them to extend your posts beyond your page and inspire people to act. Page post engagement ads provide insights into how many people liked, shared, or commented on your ad.

- Event responses - If your business is hosting an event, you can create an event announcement and page, right in the platform. Then, you can promote that event with paid advertising.
- Page likes - This ad is designed to help increase the likes on your page, and the benefit is that users are driven to your page, and then are able to learn more about your business.
- How to create a Facebook ad

Facebook provides very specific instructions to help you easily create your ad.

1. Determine your advertising objective - awareness or reach. If you are going for awareness, this means that you just want to get your ad in front of more people who will pay attention. If you are going for reach, this means that you want to get in front of as many people as you possibly can, within your budget.
2. Select your audience - Facebook lets you take what you know about your customers so that you can target your ad more effectively.
3. Decide where you want to run your ad - Facebook, Instagram, Messenger, Audience Network, or across all of them.
4. Set your budget - Facebook makes it very easy to stay within budget. You just enter your daily or lifetime budget and the time period during which you want your ads to run.

5. Pick your format - Facebook offers six ad formats that are all optimized for mobile.
6. Place your order - Submit the ad, and it goes live.
7. Measure your ad performance - Using the Facebook Ads Manager, you can track performance and edit your campaign. This is a great way to determine if one version of your ad is working better than another, or if your ad is being delivered efficiently. Based on what you learn, you can make the appropriate tweaks or adjustments.

CHAPTER 4

THE BEGINNING OF YOUTUBE

It wasn't too long after the start of Facebook that YouTube was started. Jawed Karim, Steve Chen, and Chad Hurley launched the platform in 2005, and the first YouTube video, an 18-second video that shows elephants in the background, and tells us that elephants have long trunks, was published on April 23, 2005, by Jawed Karim himself. That Me at the Zoo video, at the time of this writing, has 70,505,925 views.

Karin, Chen, and Hurley were employees of PayPal, and discovered that there was nowhere for their videos to be stored. Years later, Karim went on record to indicate that it was the Janet Jackson Super Bowl incident, and the December 2004 tsunami in the Indian Ocean that left over 225,000 dead, that triggered the idea for the platform.

After a beta testing period, and the upload of the Me at the Zoo video, the site officially launched in December 2005, with Nike being the first advertiser to upload a commercial. That Nike video was the first to receive one million views.

Since those early years, YouTube has grown exponentially. Consider these statistics:

- 1,300,000,000 people use YouTube
- Every minute, 300 hours of video are uploaded to YouTube
- 5 billion videos are watched on Youtube every day
- There are over 30 million visitors on YouTube per day
- The number of hours people spend watching videos on YouTube is up 60% year-over-year
- 9% of U.S small businesses use Youtube

YouTube Demographics

- In an average month, eight out of ten 18 to 49 year-olds watch YouTube
- 38% of YouTube users are female
- 62% of YouTube users are male
- By age, user percentages are as follows:
    - Age 18 - 24 = 11%
    - Age 25 - 34 = 23%
    - Age 35 - 44 = 26%
    - Age 45 - 54 = 16%
    - Age 50 - 64 = 8%
    - Unknown = 14%

And perhaps one of the most interesting statistics as it pertains to our purpose with this Social Media Marketing Guide, is that approximately 20% of the people who start to watch your video, will stop watching after the first ten seconds. So, while video is popular, the content has to be engaging.

YouTube Becomes a Platform for Marketers

If you are new to social media marketing, you probably don't think of YouTube as a platform for marketing use. And if you do, that's great; it means you are a step ahead of us. But while Facebook, Instagram, Twitter, and LinkedIn tend to get the most of the focus, YouTube is actually the second largest website in the world. The reach that YouTube enjoys is immense, and when used properly, it can help you to drive more traffic and engagement, which means more leads.

The Benefits of Using YouTube to Market Your Business

That iconic red play button is now well-known by internet users of all ages. And with the desire for users to watch videos instead of simply clicking through images and written content, it is no wonder that a variety of celebrities have launched their careers via YouTube.

This said, businesses of all kinds and sizes can incorporate a video marketing strategy as part of their marketing strategy.

- YouTube videos capture attention but there is a lot of competition due to the number of videos that are uploaded in any given minute - in fact, an estimated 300 hours of video are uploaded every minute!
- With over a billion users, and 5 billion videos watched on the platform every single day, there is ample opportunity to drive traffic - if your video is engaging and high quality.
- YouTube aids in viral marketing - if you embed your video link within applicable blog posts, or you share a link to a relevant video in a LinkedIn group discussion, it is highly likely that others will share your content on your behalf.
- The primary tactic to focus on with video is delivering value and insight to your followers. If your viewers find your content engaging, informative, and relevant, they will share it.

- Google acquired YouTube in 2006 for $1.65 billion in stock, as Google knew that YouTube could help them to dominate the world of search. Since YouTube videos are often ranked exceptionally high on Google's search pages, it means that a solid video marketing strategy can lead to promising SEO results.

How to Set Up a Brand Account on YouTube

Before setting up your YouTube account, open a Brand Account on Google. When you create your YouTube channel using only a regular Google account, only you can log into that channel unless you choose to share your credentials with others (and that is never a best practice). By creating your YouTube channel using a Brand Account, multiple authorized Google Accounts can log in simultaneously. You can use a Brand Account to create a channel that has a different name but that's still managed from your Google Account.

- Sign in to YouTube on a computer or using the mobile site.
- Go to your channel list.
- Choose to create a new channel or use an existing Brand Account:
    - Create a new channel by clicking on Create a new channel.
    - Create a YouTube channel for a Brand Account that you already manage by choosing the Brand Account from the list. If this Brand Account already has a channel, you can't create a new one—you'll just be switched over to that channel if you select the Brand Account from the list.
- Fill out the details to name your new channel and verify your account.

- Then, click Done. This will create your new Brand Account.
- To add a channel manager, follow the instructions to change channel owners and managers.

Now, you are ready to set up your YouTube brand account. Note that your personal Google account will automatically give you a personal YouTube account. But, if you are setting up the YouTube account for your business, you will want a brand account. With a personal account, only you will be able to access it.

When creating a YouTube brand account, you will be able to customize your channel for your brand and give access to other members of your marketing team. It's important to determine who will get access to the YouTube account before you get too far in the process, as it will be important to assign roles and responsibilities and to manage expectations. Granting access to various members of your marketing team will allow them to help manage the channel through their own Google accounts as well. So, when you grant access to a Google account in YouTube, there will be three different options for team member roles:

- Owners have full editing power over all of your company's Google properties. Owners can add or remove managers, edit business information, respond to reviews, and more.
- Managers have the same editing powers as Owners, with the exception that they cannot add or remove page roles or remove listings. Anyone editing a YouTube channel must be a Manager or an Owner.
- Communications Managers can respond to reviews and do a handful of other actions but they cannot use YouTube's video manager, upload content, or view analytics.

Now that you understand the various roles available to your team, do the following:

- Log into YouTube using your Google brand account details.
- Go to your YouTube channels page. If you've never created a YouTube channel before, you'll only see your personal account. If you already have an existing brand channel, you'll see it as well. To create a new brand channel, click Create a new channel.

Next, add your brand identity. Remember that your YouTube channel is an extension of your company's brand and it is imperative that it is treated as such by all employees. As you create and customize your channel, you can leverage these YouTube brand guidelines so you can establish your channel's identity and begin to attract subscribers. This is a critical step anytime you are setting up a social channel for your company.

- Log into YouTube on a computer. Note that you can only edit your channel images from a computer, and not from a mobile device.
- Click your profile icon on the top right of the screen and choose Your channel.
- Hover above the profile image to bring up the Edit channel icon function. Upload an image or channel icon (ideally your company logo), and adjust the cropping as appropriate. The recommended image size is 800 x 800 pixels, and it will render at 98 x 98 pixels on YouTube. This image will be used across all of your Google properties such as Gmail and Google+. Consider using a company logo or, if you are a public figure, a professional headshot.
- Hover above the banner image to bring up the Edit channel art function. The recommended image size is 2,560 x 1,440 pixels.

Here are some other helpful hints:

- Your channel name is associated with each video that you publish for your brand. Make sure that it is correct as well as consistent with your other social media sites and overall branding.
- Your description should provide more information on your company and explain what type of video content you plan to share with users. Search engines will look at your description when determining how to rank your profile, so be sure to incorporate relevant keywords in your overview. Refer to the Leveraging SEO in Your Marketing Efforts in this guide for a refresher on keyword strategy.
- Your trailer should be 30 to 60 seconds in length and should focus on showing visitors what your channel is about and what they can expect to see in your videos. Be sure to include that call to action that encourages them to subscribe to your channel.
- Your channel may be eligible for a custom URL once your company has over 100 subscribers, a channel icon, channel art, and is more than 30 days old.
- Link to all of your company's other social media accounts and relevant websites from the "About" section of your channel. You must make it easy for subscribers to connect with you anywhere that your company can be found online.

Now you can add links to your YouTube channel banner.

- Log into YouTube on a computer, and go to your channel. Click Customize channel.
- Click on the About tab, then scroll down to Links.
- Click the pencil icon so that you can add links, which will appear over your channel banner art.

- Enter your company's website information, and add links to your company's other social channels (these will be indicated with social media icons).

Congratulations! You are now ready to upload your first video. However, in the case of your business, the Me at the Zoo video is not a model that you should try to follow. Make sure that you have high quality, top of the funnel content, for use.

To upload a video:

- Sign into your YouTube account.
- Click on the Create a Video or Post button at the top of your screen.
- Click Upload video.
- Select the video you'd like to upload from your computer.
- Add a title up to 100 characters and a description up to 5,000 characters. Include keywords in your description, but don't go overboard. Keyword stuffing is never a good practice.
- Click Publish.

The Rise of Video in Marketing

Today's marketers are discovering that video is an invaluable tool, as it heightens brand awareness, and engages prospects. Consider these statistics as I shared in the Instagram Marketing Guide 2021:

- 55% of people watch videos online every day
- 92% of mobile video consumers share videos with others

- 90% of users say that product videos are helpful in the decision process, and after watching a video, 64% of users are more likely to buy a product online
- Social video generates 1200% more shares than text and images combined
- 80% of users recall a video ad they viewed in the past 30 days

Additionally, according to Hubspot, more than 50% of consumers want to see videos from the brands that they love. So, digital marketers need to strive to produce and distribute content that engages and resonates. While video is definitely more expensive to produce, when done correctly, the return on investment will quickly present itself.

On Facebook alone, video posts get 135% greater reach than static images. And, after consumers have viewed a video, they often provide reactions and comments right then, which increases your ability to communicate with them. According to a 2018 article in Forbes, companies using video content experience a traffic increase of 41% in web searches compared to marketers who don't include video content in their marketing strategy. Not only that, when consumers love your video, they are highly likely to share it with others.

Optimizing your YouTube Video for SEO

When creating videos for YouTube, it is important that they are properly optimized. The first step you need to take is to create and optimize your video's metadata. Metadata provides viewers with important information about your video, such as your video title, description, tags, category, thumbnail, subtitles, and closed captions.

When you have the correct information included in your video's metadata, it ensures that the video will be properly indexed by YouTube and that the video will appear when people are searching for videos similar to yours. Be concise and straightforward when filling out your metadata. In fact, your content could be removed if you try to promote it with unrelated keywords.

- Title - As I have discussed, just as with on-page SEO, it's important to optimize your video's title and description. People read the title first when they are scrolling through a list of videos. Make sure your video title is both clear and compelling. Your title should make those searching for content curious about what your video will do to help them solve their problem. Conduct keyword research to understand what viewers are searching for. Include the most important information and keywords in the beginning of your title, and keep titles to approximately 60 characters so that text does not get cut off in results pages.
- Description - YouTube will only display about 100 characters of your video's description. If viewers want to read on, they will need to click "Show more" to see the rest. So, include important links or CTAs in the beginning of your description and prepare the copy so that is will be compelling enough to drive views and engagement.
- Tags - Highlight your main keywords in your tags. Tags associate your video with similar videos, which broadens its reach. Tag your most important keywords first and try to include a suitable mix of more common keywords as well as long-tail keywords.
- Category - You can sort your video into one of the following categories:
    - Film & Animation
    - Autos & Vehicles

- Comedy
- Gaming
- Music
- Pets & Animals
- Sports
- Travel & Events
- People & Blogs
- Entertainment
- News & Politics
- How-to & Style
- Education
- Science & Technology
- Nonprofits & Activism

- Thumbnail - Create a great thumbnail image from your video. When you have a good thumbnail, more people will click, and that will result in better SEO.
- Add subtitles and closed-captioning for ADA compliance as well as to help aid in search results.

The Use of Video Across the Sales Funnel

While there are various versions of the sales funnel in use throughout the world, most of them follow a similar approach. The sales funnel, from top to bottom, usually looks like this:

- Awareness - this is where your prospects become aware of your company, product, or service
- Interest - Your prospects starts to show interest in what you have to offer
- Evaluation - Your prospect is comparing what you have to offer versus your competition

- Decision or Desire - Your prospect wants what you have to offer, and is ready to make a decision
- Purchase or Action - The nurturing process has converted, and the customer has engaged in a transaction
- Reevaluation - If your product is a consumable (like a cupcake) or needs to be renewed or upgraded on a regular basis, this is when your prospect turned customer decides if they want to do business with you again
- Repurchase - The customer decides to keep the relationship intact, and purchases from you again

The top of the sales funnel is about building brand awareness. Typical videos to use to help people learn about your organization and to associate your brand with the service or product you offer, include:

- Brand videos - This can be a quick overview of your company, a high-level video that shows your employees at work or doing something good in the community, or a core values video
- Educational and how-to videos - This is an opportunity to educate viewers about the service or product you sell. For a cupcake shop, this is an opportunity to show a video of one of the bakers going through the baking process for a cupcake. Or, this could be a video with a cupcake shop employee making their favorite cupcake recipe.
- Interviews with influencers and thought leaders - Demonstrating thought leadership in your niche is important. This isn't about trying to sell directly, or a "our company does this," type message. Rather, this is an opportunity to share a perspective about something related to your business, without directly talking about your business. For our

cupcake shop, this could be the owner of the cupcake shop talking about enjoying sweets in moderation, or about how to maintain a green work environment in the baking business.

- Animated videos - Animation is very popular in marketing. While it should not be the only format that you use, the incorporation of on-brand animated videos enables a faster-to-market video strategy, that is often easier to update or modify if a part of your business changes and messages need to be updated.
- Documentaries - This could be a video that tells the story of how your business came to be. Or, if you are in the service industry, it could be the story of someone whose life was made better because of the services you provided.

The middle of the sales funnel focuses on lead nurturing, which is all about keeping your audience interested so that they can learn more about who you are and how you can make their life, or their business, better. Videos to use in the middle of the sales funnel include:

- Product videos - These are demo videos that show how your product or service is used.
- Video (customer) testimonials – These videos are similar to case studies, but include the actual customer, talking about the benefits that your service or product provided.
- Case studies – These videos explain how a client or customer benefited from your product or service. Case studies can be very beneficial for prospective clients that will want to check your references, or be reassured that others have been happy to work with you.

- Video blogs - Created daily or weekly, these videos document the daily life of your employees at work or events that your company participates in . You can also record a video that summarizes or highlights a blog post so your audience has multiple ways to digest the content.
- Event videos - These are filmed at events and trade-shows that your company may be sponsoring or attending. Videoing these in-person experiences at a conference or expo can be a great way to show the excitement of a crowd, and to alert attendees that you are there (or that you were there).

The bottom of the sales funnel is where we want to see customers convert, and engage in a transaction. This means that they are well educated, and we want them to be ready and confident to buy. Consider these suggestions:

- Competition scorecard videos - These videos should not necessarily name your competition, but should highlight and showcase what makes your service or product different than that of your competitors. For the cupcake shop, this could be a comparison of ingredients. Perhaps your cupcakes are 30 less calories than the closest competitor. Or, maybe your cupcakes are 20% bigger for the same price. This is an opportunity to compare and contrast what your business has, that others do not.
- In-depth product demo / explainer video - This video is a follow-on to the product video that is developed for middle of the funnel marketing. In this video, you get far deeper into the weeds, and more thoroughly discuss what your buyer needs to know.

Tips & Tricks of YouTube Marketing

If you plan to use video in your social media marketing strategy, and I highly recommend that you do, it is important to stay up to date and the latest trends and strategies. These tips below are intended to help you get started to ensure that your YouTube video strategy is the best it can be. And, keep in mind that with YouTube, it can be a powerful marketing platform as a stand-alone, but when you combine your TubeTube marketing efforts with your strategy on other platforms, it will be that much more impactful.

1. Be authentic - Your users want simplicity. If you overdo it, you'll likely alienate your audience, and they will be far less likely to watch another video. Your viewers want to create a relationship and a connection with your brand, so make sure that your video is genuine.

2. Use storytelling - Storytelling is probably the most powerful way that you can make your brand come alive, and is a key to content marketing. When you tell a story about your product or service, you give it an identity that can resonate with the target audience within your niche. Stories are what create connections.

3. Don't make your video a be all and end all video. One video is not going to satisfy your audience, especially if you try to do too much. So, don't try to make one video cover your company overview, core values, and a benefits list of all of the products that you have to offer. That's too much. Keep it simple, and your message will better resonate.

4. For social media, shorter videos are better. Of course, this doesn't mean that you can't have a 10-minute video. You just need to be thoughtful and how long you can hold the attention space of your audience. This is especially important at the top of the funnel when you are trying to make a good impression. If you put out a 15-minute video about your company, your audience will close the video

and move on to something else. Leverage this guidance from wistia.com.

- o Videos up to two minutes long get tons of engagement
- o Engagement experiences a significant drop-off between two and three minutes
- o Videos that are six to 12 minutes in length are the next ideal - but again, this is not for those top of funnel pieces. This longer-form content is better served at the middle and bottom of the funnel.
- o Be cautious on any video over 12 minutes in length. Reserve this for technical demonstration type videos where the audience will expect that type of a deep-dive, and will more likely be engaged for the entire piece.

5. Include a call-to-action at the end of your video. If you have excited your audience, what do you want them to do? On YouTube, as on other forms of social media, you can include a clickable button in your messaging that will take your audience to your website, or the designated place where they can learn more. And, on the video itself, ensure that your brand logo is included, and that your company name and website address show up whenever it makes sense, and in the least, at the end of the video.

6. Promote your YouTube video on all of your social media platforms. Write short bits of copy that can be leveraged for each platform, and then push the video out across channels so that you can reach as many of the target audience members in your niche as possible. And just because you posted it once, doesn't mean you shouldn't post it again. In fact, you should promote your various videos regularly across social media platforms, co-mingled with other original and curated content that makes sense for your audience.

Leveraging SEO in Your Marketing Efforts

Another thing to remember with YouTube marketing is the concept of search engine optimization (SEO). If you are not yet familiar with SEO, it is the practice of increasing the quality and quantity of traffic to your website. In doing so, this means increased exposure for your brand through non-paid (aka organic) search engine results.

SEO is about both people and search engines. When SEO is done correctly, it means that you have properly assessed what people are searching for online, the questions that they are asking, and how these are asking those questions to get the answers that they seek. If you know how a customer is going to ask a question, you can ensure that your content includes that language, so that it can be more easily located during web searches.

Search engines crawl (thus why you might hear the term web crawler) the internet and discover and catalog the information that they come across. So, in this order, you want to ensure that your content addresses the following:

1. Crawl accessibility so engines can easily reach and index your content
2. Compelling and informative content that answers the searcher's questions
3. Keyword optimization to attract both potential customers (searchers) and engines
4. A fast load speed, ease of use, and compelling user interface regardless of device used
5. Content that people want to share, which will earn links, citations, and amplification
6. Title, URL, and description to draw high click through rates in search rankings

7. Ability to stand out in search engine results pages (SERPs)

Thus, for YouTube specifically, you should consider it as a search engine for videos. And since YouTube acts as its own search engine, it has its own suggested best practices for SEO. Here is a list of techniques that will help you get the visibility that you desire for your YouTube content.

- Keywords are very important on YouTube. Leverage Google's keyword planner to check your list of keywords to see how often they are searched for. Your keywords should represent your business and your video content to help the YouTube platform understand what your channel or content is about. But, if the Google planner is not showing many hits on the keywords you think are important, then you need to go back to the drawing board. Ideally, your selected video keywords should get you several hundred searches each month. If you are struggling to come up with great keywords, look at the keywords used by your competitors for ideas.
- Your video headline and description need to be optimized by using relevant keywords in both the headline and your video description. Not only that, you should try to solve a problem in your headline. It is for this reason that so many YouTube video titles start with "How to."
- Good metadata is paramount for a successful YouTube channel. Along with your optimized YouTube video titles and descriptions, you need to have a tagging strategy. With the right tags in place, your videos will rank higher in search and will more often surface as suggested videos on YouTube. 10 to 12 tags per video should suffice.
- Ask your viewers to comment by adding a call to action at the end of your video. Ask a question to

start a conversation. Or, simply ask people to comment.

- Seek subscribers. Liking or commenting on a video is a one-time action, but when a follower subscribes to your channel, that means that they will see your content on a regular basis, and will be more likely to share it with other followers. The more time people spend watching your videos, the better your SEO will be. YouTube will promote videos that get people to watch for a longer time, rather than videos that are opened and closed quickly.
- Don't go cheap on video production. Make sure your videos are well planned and are created well. Ensure people can clearly see the video and that they can understand what is being said. This doesn't mean that you need to spend thousands of dollars on videos. But, you do need to take the time to create a high-quality video that people will want to watch.
- Create a great thumbnail image from your video. When you have a good thumbnail, more people will click, and that will result in better SEO.
- Add closed-captioning. Not only is this ADA compliant, but it is also great for people who watch videos with the sound turned off on their device. Above and beyond that, closed captions are crawlable and can be found by search engines.
- Make sure that your filename is updated from your standard file nomenclature used in your organization. Use your keyword in the title and enough information to tell viewers what the video is about.
- Embed links back to your website, and not just to your other videos.

- Share your videos on social media (refer to our section titled Tips & Tricks of YouTube Marketing). Facebook, Twitter, LinkedIn, and Instagram are all great places to share your business's YouTube content.

- If you have an email marketing strategy, include a short story about your video in your next email newsletter, and make sure you include a link so that they can be taken to the video.

- Embed your video in your blog posts as applicable.

- Increase your viewer watch time by adding some suspense to your videos. You can ask a question at the beginning that is answered at the end, or even share a statistic at the beginning that people will want to learn more about. But whatever you do, don't create a cliffhanger statement that isn't actually addressed in the video. We've all seen articles with titles or photos that capture our attention, and then we read through and either find out the photo had nothing to do with the article, or that they completely altered the title to capture attention and the article had nothing to do with the title - don't be that marketer.

- Find the optimal video length that works for your customers. In most cases, videos up to three minutes in length will get the best engagement. Refer back to our section on Tips & Tricks of YouTube Marketing for more information on optimal video length.

CHAPTER 5

THE BEGINNING OF TWITTER

Not long after Facebook and YouTube, Twitter co-founder Jack Dorsey had an idea for what would become Twitter, in 2006. Dorsey had originally envisioned Twitter as an SMS-based platform for communications. The ideas was that groups of friends could stay connected by keeping tabs on what each other were doing based on their status updates. So, a bit like texting, but not really. And a bit like Faceboom, but not really.

During a brainstorming session at Odeo, a podcasting company, Dorsey pitched his idea for this SMS-based platform to the Odeo co-founder Evan Williams. Evan and his co-founder Biz Stone gave Dorsey the go-ahead to keep working on the project and to develop it further.

In the beginning, Twitter was referred to as twttr. At the time that Twitter came out, it was popular to drop vowels in the name of their companies and services, and this was believed to be a competitive advantage. Software genius Noah Glass was eventually credited with coming up with the original name twttr, and eventually, Twitter.

The first tweet was sent by Dorsey, from Twitter, on March 21, 2006, and it read, "just setting up my twttr."

By 2007, the South by Southwest Interactive conference was underway, and it experienced a huge explosion of Twitter usage, with over 60,000 tweets sent each day of the event. The Twitter team was in attendance at the event, and leveraged the viral nature of the opportunity to grow the app's popularity.

While Twitter experienced a variety of ups and downs during the early years, the user base grew swiftly. And, developers even got creative when servers found themselves overloaded, featuring the illustration of a whale being lifted out of the water (an illustration by artist Yiying Lu) by eight birds. This image appeared on the screen of Twitter followers, as a creative way to tell users that Twitter was "working on it." This whale become known as the fail whale.

Just How Many Characters can be in a Twitter Tweet?

When the platform launched, there was a character limit of 140, which was simply based on SMS protocol. And, as Twitter continued to grow, that 140 character limit simply became part of the Twitter brand. In 2017, Twitter evolved with the smartphone age (albeit a bit late) and increased the tweet size limit to 280 characters. While some Twitter users balked at the change, it was generally accepted as a positive change. And, Twitter shared with users that most tweets are about 50 characters as it is, so the change simply allows for more characters as needed.

The character increase actually helps to increase the flow of communication on Twitter, as users can now spend less time figuring out how to state their message in 140 characters or less, and can more quickly get their message out to followers.

Interestingly, as the Twitter user base began to grow, users started creating their own jargon, and even inventing ways to use the platform. In the beginning, there was no way to reply to other users on Twitter. So, tech-savvy users started to include the @ symbol before a username, to indicate a response to a particular user, within a tweet. Before long, more and more users caught on, and eventually the Twitter team added this functionality as a native option within the application. A similar thing happened with hashtags (more on hashtags later), and later with retweets. For retweets in particular, users sought a way to repost a message from a user, while including credit to that user who had originally tweeted it. So, again, those tech savvy users found a way to solve for the problem, and began adding RT before sending a message. This RT would become a signal to followers that the tweet was a retweet. In 2010, Twitter formally added this functionality to the application.

As an additional quick note on retweets, if you want your followers to retweet your tweet, you should blatantly ask them to do so. Tweets that actually ask followers to retweet receive 12 times more retweets than those that do not. Seems almost too good to be true, but it does indeed work.

While Twitter growth has slowed in recent years, the application still has a reported 321 million monthly users. And, Twitter has indicated that the reason for the decline in their active user base is because as an organization, they are cracking down on fake accounts. Getting rid of these bad accounts is a wise strategy for Twitter, and one that users will benefit from, as it means that the platform is comprised of more real users.

How to Set Up a Business Account on Twitter

- Go to Twitter.com and sign up. Use your real name and your real email address, and set-up a password. Note that you will be able to customize your profile later.
    - Note: Twitter only allows one account per email. So, if you have a personal Twitter account,

you will need to use a different email to set up your business Twitter account.

- Join Twitter by completing the form with your name, your email, a password, and a username. This is where you can change your username.
- Click "create my account".
- Click "next".
- Build your timeline. Twitter asks you to follow 3 people from a selection it gives you. You must follow 3 people from this selection.
- Twitter will then ask you to follow 5 more, and then 5 people you know. It is suggested that you follow employees within your organization, or other key businesses that serve your niche or target audience. If preferred, skip these last two steps by clicking on the "skip" button on the bottom right hand side of the box.
- Twitter will then ask you confirm your email address. Check your email for confirmation, and then click on the link in the email from Twitter.
- Your Twitter account is now ready, and you can begin to customize your Twitter profile and page. When customizing your Twitter account, keep your handle, profile photo, background image and bio consistent with your company brand, and social media marketing strategy.
- Upload your profile image, which will be called your avatar. This photo is how you appear in your Tweets to your followers and it gives your account an identity. The maximum file size for your photo is 700MB, and it is best to use your company logo.
- Upload your header. The header will show up as the background to your Twitter photo (your company

logo). It shows up on mobile too, so it is important to include this in your Twitter account. The recommended dimensions for a header are 1252 x 626, with maximum file size of 5MB

- Add your business website so that Twitter followers can easily click through to your website. Note that as you develop more followers on Twitter, and you are using Twitter to market certain social sites, or special promotions, you can change always change this website to direct your Twitter traffic to particular landing pages.
- Add your bio. You have 160 characters to work with.
- Click "Save Changes."
- To see your completed Twitter profile, click on "Me" in the top header.
- You are now ready to send your company's first Tweet.

The Scoop with the Hashtag

While I discussed the use of hashtags in our Instagram Marketing Guide 2021, it's wise to provide a refresher here, especially since the hashtag actually started with Twitter. So, let's make sure you understand what hashtags are, as these are critical in helping you to stay on trend and to grow your followers.

But first, I'll give just a bit of history on the hashtag now that I am talking about Twitter marketing. Chris Messina, a well-known social technology (and now social media) expert, has been credited with using the very first hashtag on Twitter. In August 2007, he proposed the use of the hashtag as a way to add organization to tweets. It didn't take long for the concept to take off, and in July 2009, the hashtag was made an official feature. Facebook followed in 2013.

If you're not clear on what hashtags are, hashtags leverage keywords or phrases that are placed together without spaces and then are preferred with that # symbol. In most cases, they are used to reference events, key goings-on in the entertainment industry, or recurring themes.

Development of your hashtag strategy is critical to creating engagement with your followers. In fact, it is believed that the use of a hashtag will increase engagement by more than 10%. Effective use of a hashtag can and will help you to increase your followers.

Every tweet can use as many hashtags as you want, but Twitter recommends no more than two hashtags per tweet.

You can use a hashtag whenever you're referring to a specific topic. For instance, you could use hashtags for:

1. Events: #TrumpVisitsQueen, #WorldSeries
2. Places: #Aruba, #Paris, #beautiful places
3. Themes: #ThursdayThoughts
4. Things: #coffee, #computers, #cars, #cupcakes
5. Verbs: #singing, #reading, #writing
6. Industry terms: #socialmedia, #photography, #tech

So, in our repeated illustration of our cupcake shop, consider tweets that add #bestcupcakesinseattle or #cupcake.

There are a variety of different styles of hashtags, based on what you are trying to accomplish.

1. Branded hashtags are specific to your company and could be your company name or tagline.
2. Community hashtags are intended to connect users around a specific subject and similar interests. The #bestcupcakesinseattle and #cupcake hashtags mentioned above are great examples as they

indirectly refer to your brand in that they are about cupcakes and enjoying cupcakes in Seattle.

3. Campaign hashtags are used for a specific campaign, and only for a short duration of time. So, if our cupcake shop had a special month-long promotion with a new flavor every day for 30 days, a suitable hashtag might be #30daycupcakechallenge.

Be careful when developing your hashtags to not get too general. While the #cupcakes hashtag works, it is pretty broad, and if you search for #cupcakes on Twitter, you will get a LOT of hits.

Also, check what hashtags your influencers (or ideal influencers) are using. Since these people are spokespersons for various industries, they are viewed as experts in the space, and perform well on social media, partially due to how and what hashtags they use to draw in more and more followers.

The 25 Most Popular Hashtags on Twitter

According to Hubspot, these are the 25 best hashtags to get likes on a tweet:

1. ico
2. ethereum
3. crypto
4. crowdfunding
5. medicaid
6. blackhistorymonth
7. womenshistorymonth
8. photography
9. iwd2018
10. cryptocurrency

11. happyeaster
12. womensday
13. pressforprogress
14. happybirthday
15. internationalwomensday
16. olympics
17. pets
18. friends
19. piday
20. worldwaterday
21. funny
22. contest
23. starwarsday
24. giveaway
25. tuesdaymotivation

Twitter Becomes a Platform for Marketers

Twitter, while it is definitely unique in how to engage, is absolutely free for marketers. This provides a unique opportunity, especially as it compares to other social media platforms. The key here is to understand that Twitter can not and should not be the only social channel where you market your brand. Rather, use Twitter to do the following:

- Connect with your customers - If a customer makes a comment about their experience with your brand on Twitter, it is very easy to respond quickly either publically, or via a personal message. And, if they start to follow-you, sending them a quick personal message can really help to bolster future loyalty, as well as trust and appreciation. Customers want to feel appreciated, and when you take the time to give them attention, it can really pay off.

- Stay on top of the competition - When customers lodge a complaint on a competitor site, you want to know how they are responding. Marketers should make note of this activity and share it with the leadership team as part of their competitive intelligence strategy. You can even get ideas for future content for Twitter and Facebook marketing by looking at the problems that customers are posting on Twitter. Turn that information into a "how to" type article, or an acknowledgement of some of the problems or concerns in your industry.
- Keep your customers up to date - Twitter provides an excellent vehicle to inform your customers of sales and promotions, or even to share relevant articles from your industry.
- Establish a line of communication - Provide product release or technical support updates via Twitter. The platform can be used for far more than marketing messages.
- Build a community - You can use Twitter to create smaller communities, or pockets of users that can help you with retweets and favoring of content. This practice will help you to get more visibility so that you can acquire more customers. And, these communities can work much like a focus group or survey panel by providing you with helpful information that your product development colleagues can use to improve your products and services.

Increase sales - Over half of a brand's followers are more likely to perform an initial or repeat purchase after they have followed the brand on Twitter. This means that

Twitter is a marketing platform that can actually pay off by helping you to grow your sales and revenue.

Today's business owners are encouraged to engage on Twitter. And loyal fans and followers can help you to increase your visibility and stay on top of the competition. While there are far less Twitter users than there are Facebook users, businesses around the globe still view Twitter as a valuable asset in their online marketing strategy.

Increasing your Engagement on Twitter

Social media really is a popularity contest. Everyone is on Twitter these days, including your friends and family, your favorite celebrities, and your favorite brand. So if you want to get followers fast and increase your followers fast, try these suggestions:

1. Promote your presence on Twitter in all of your assets including print media (such as a Follow Us on Twitter message with Twitter icon) and digital media. If people don't know that you are on Twitter, they can't follow you there. Include your Twitter handle wherever you can, including on business cards, physical printed flyers, magazine or newspaper ads, etc. For digital media, do the same but ensure the media is hyperlinked to your Twitter channel so that readers can simply click and access.
2. Tweet frequently. In fact, if you have the resources to do so, you should be tweeting anywhere from one to 30 times per day, as long as the content is relevant and engaging.
3. Promote your Twitter (and other social handles) at the end of your company's blog posts. Embed your live Twitter feed to your blog's website and make sure there is a Twitter follow button on your site as well. Adding a "Tweet this" button will make sharing

your blog with others easier, and will be sure to help increase engagement.

4. Reply to Tweets publically. If your customers are tweeting on your account, be sure to respond and tweet back. Don't resort to the personal message unless it is absolutely necessary.

5. Make sure that you are sharing relevant and engaging content. You should share content from your own website, such as blogs, whitepapers, and articles, but you should also be sharing relevant curated content. And, tweets that tell a story will earn your business more followers than those that do not, as they are more engaging.

6. Trendjacking, which is along the lines of sharing curated content. is a great way to generate awareness for yourself or brand. But, if you are not careful, it can backfire. Trendjacking, when done appropriately, is when you chime in on relevant business conversations with authentic commentary. But, if your brand isn't about being edgy, then don't try to be. Search trends for opportunities to chime in with your company's opinion on a popular industry article or regarding a hot-button issue. And, make sure to always stay civil and to ensure you are not commenting on any topics that are taboo according to your company's social media policy.

7. Don't be afraid to use emojis in your posts. In fact, this is true for all social media platforms. It is proven that social posts with more than just text content can get more engagement. Being able to make a trending meme mesh with your talking points is one way you can end up with a viral tweet of your own. But, you really have to have to understand your target audience to pull this off. A poorly executed meme can seriously damage your brand. On the other hand, GIFs are easier and less risky to use, but

they can still make your brand look bad if you use them incorrectly. Thankfully, Twitter has a GIF button that makes it easy to find a relevant GIF. Emojis are the least useful in the context of Twitter for SEO ranking, but they can be helpful in adding more emotional context to your Tweets, which improves engagement.

CHAPTER 6

WHEN TO POST

As you will learn now that you are studying the benefits and strategies for various social media platforms, social media is always changing, as are user behaviors. So, while there isn't an exact science on when to post your content, studies have been done to show when posts are more likely to generate interest and engagement.

If your company adopts a process of posting content when users aren't engaged, your users will quickly pick up on the fact that you are not tuned in with who they are. And, with marketing automation technologies, it is easy to schedule content in advance so that it is set to release at the right time of day, on the right day of the week, to ensure you are maximizing your exposure.

When to Post on Facebook

Of all social media platforms, Facebook has the highest level of engagement. Content that drives genuine interest and engagement is most likely to be successful. The best times for your business to post content on Facebook are:

- Wednesday at 11 AM and 1 PM

- Weekdays in general from 9AM to 3PM
- Early mornings and evenings, before 7 AM and after 5PM have the least amount of engagement per day, as people are either sleeping or engaging with family and friends
- Sunday has the least amount of engagement for Facebook

Remember that many people check their phones immediately upon waking in the morning, which provides a great idea to plant some content in their minds before they go about their day, thus why 7AM or later is wise. Also, people tend to visit social sites during the workday vs. after work or on the weekends when they are more likely engaged in family and fun activities.

In most cases, engagement on Mondays is relatively low as people are returning to work after a weekend off. People tend to check their social media accounts during their lunch breaks, and again during the late afternoon when energy levels start to fade after a long day at work. On the weekends, Saturday mornings tend to be active as parents check in while their kids are off at various activities.

As you have reviewed the above information, a natural follow-on question is regarding time zones. In this case, it is important to understand the time zone that is most prevalent for your target audience. So, if your primary audience is on the east coast, then, you should use the eastern time zone and apply it to the directional guidance provided above.

If your followers tend to be geographically dispersed, you may want to create a time zone map that shows the various locations of your audience, and then look for windows of potential overlap so that some of your posts can be multi-purpose, serving more than one time zone at once.

When to Post on Twitter

Timeliness is critical for Twitter, as there are 500 million tweets sent per day. The challenge with Twitter, however, is that is tends to highlight activity out of order based on the interests of its followers. So, posting at off-peak hours could cause you to miss out on significant amount of engagement.

- The best times are on Wednesday at 9 AM and Friday at 9 AM
- Tuesdays and Wednesdays are best
- On Mondays, post between 8AM to 4PM, and while people are often getting caught up at work, Twitter provides a great opportunity for professionals to also catch up on the news they need to know for the week, and Twitter can be a great source
- Saturday has the lowest levels of engagement
- In general, it is best to avoid between the hours of 10 PM and 4 AM when people are sleeping - tweets that take place during this window will most likely be missed entirely

CHAPTER 7

THE IMPORTANCE OF INFLUENCERS

As I stated in the Instagram Marketing Guide 2021, an influencer strategy is one where a marketer relies heavily (but not primarily) on others to aid in building brand awareness, building authority, and connecting with more users. These influencers help drive traffic to your business website and can result in increased conversion rates and additional followers of your brand.

Influencer marketing can drive an estimated 11x return-on-investment (ROI) over the traditional digital marketing channels, or even a social media strategy that doesn't leverage an influencer approach. In most cases, an influencer strategy is developed by identifying someone who has a strong influence on your industry or on your target audience. Your brand then forms a relationship with that influencer and the influencer agrees to expose their followers to your brand's messaging and content.

Again, using our example of a cupcake shop, let's consider the impact of a celebrity and authority figure such as Buddy Valastro (Cake Boss), on the positive impact his support could have on your business. Now, we understand that most companies can't afford Buddy as their influencer, so we're simply using this for illustrative purposes, as we know that he is a famous baker, and is regularly featured on talk shows and cooking shows.

If your cupcake store released a new product line of bakeware that is interesting to Buddy, and he agrees to promote your bakeware over a series of posts over a determined period of time, tagging your business, this would inevitably result in additional visits to your website, and more and more users following you officially, and making purchases of your products online. It could also mean higher foot traffic coming into your shop to order cupcakes, or purchase those products from you directly.

Another example of celebrity influence is that of singer, Rhianna. She has more than 86 million followers, and when she isn't occupied making music, she is busy collaborating with brands such as Fenty and Stance, and connecting with politicians to ask them to prioritize girls' education.

So again, this is an extreme example, and influencers like Buddy and Rhianna carry a price tag that most brands can't support. But, there are a variety of influencers with substantial audiences that are ready, able, and wanting to help you promote your brand, at a rate that is much more palatable for your business's budget.

How to find influencers that your business can afford

To find the right influencer for your brand, you need to go back to your target audience as you want your influencers to share the same target audience. Thinking of your target audience and your personas, who represents your brand?

- A cool and trendy college-aged girl?
- A college-aged boy?
- A tech-savvy businessman?
- A middle-class mom of two?

- A thrifty DIYer?
- A single career-minded female looking to make her next career move?

Now that you know the type of influencer you want, consider that the right influencer has a lot of followers but those followers are engaged. Dig deep by looking at how these influencers' followers are interacting with the brand. Are they sharing comments? Videos? Are you seeing anything that goes against your brand's core values or that might offend a strong portion of your customers?

Certainly, life does happen, and even influencers with the best of intentions can find themselves in the middle of an online brawl. Know that this can happen, but that you should look for influencers that are as close as possible in their values to yours. 61% of marketers in the United States have indicated that it is challenging to find the right influencer for their brand, so understand that you are not alone here. And, many marketers share concerns about the impact of influencers to brand safety.

The common challenges of an influencer marketing strategy

So before I share some suggested platforms to help you identify your influencer(s), let's review the typical concerns that marketers have with their influencer strategies. While in no means does this list below suggest you should not proceed, it is important to enter any influencer relationship with your eyes wide open.

According to a January 2021 survey titled "Leading influencer marketing challenges according to U.S. marketers," by Mediakix, the following was discovered:

- 50% of marketers share concerns about spotting fake followers and inauthentic engagement
- 41% of marketers indicated that they are building an always-on strategy rather than proceeding with one-off campaigns

- 38% of marketers cited challenges with rising influencer costs
- 33% of marketers shared that it is challenging to keep up with social media trends to stay relevant
- 33% of marketers shared concerns about building a strong creative strategy
- 30% of marketers shared the need to reduce the amount of time spent on marketing campaigns
- 28% of marketers shared challenges with brand safety and brand alignment
- 18% of marketers shared concerns with federal trade commission (FTC) regulations and requirements
- 17% of marketers indicated that they are tapping into additional channels such as Twitch
- 12% of marketers indicated that they are moving influencer marketing in-house

Finding your influencers

Influencers come in all shapes and sizes, online that is. Let's start by understanding the levels of influencers so that you can determine the type that is right for you.

1. Nano-influencers - The first tier of influencers is referred to as nano-influencers. Marketers are more and more often giving changes to those with less followers than the traditional influencers. These influencers have 1,000 to 5,000 followers on their account, and their followers are typically friends and others who share similar interests. In this case, it is not about followers idolizing those people, but rather, just being interested in what they have to say because they share a similar interest or passion. And a strong population of marketers (nearly half)

feel that the audience relationship is the key factor in whether or not an influencer will be successful.

These influencers are considered highly approachable and are thereby very lucrative to marketers, especially those will a limited budget. These influencers come across as more trustworthy because their followers feel like their advice is genuine, and it feels like they are getting advice from a friend. Nano-influencers are also easier to contact and collaborate with as there are far fewer strings in the relationship.Usually, these influencers will promote your product for a nominal fee, or a free product from your brand.

1. Micro-influencers - This next tier of influencers is a group that has between 5,000 to 20,000 followers (note that some marketers view this group as having 2,000 to 50,000 followers, and in these cases, they are simply looking at fewer tiers than what I am sharing here in this guide). These influencers are very well informed and are often experts on a particular topic. Further, they have a very engaged community of followers who are looking to the influencers to provide content that they can trust. These believe gain credibility through their authenticity because they are everyday people sharing what they like and what they don't.

2. Mid-tier influencers - This middle tier has 20,000 to 100,000 followers. Their audiences are mid-sized, as the category implies, yet they generate very high engagement rates and higher engagement rates than micro-influencers.

3. Macro-influencers - This tier has 100,000 to 1,000,000 followers. These influencers are generally well known in their communities and have dedicated audiences that have grown over time. Their content is very high in quality and is focused on something that the macro-influencer is passionate for. Marketers often like working with

macro-influencers as they are far more affordable than the next tier, and their content is rarely impacted by algorithms that limit who feeds get to. As such, these influencers have very good reach which results in very good engagement. In many cases, macro-influencers product their content using professional equipment, and these professionals have taken time to hone their craft and their tone of voice.

4. Mega-influencers - These influencers are just that, mega, with an impressive following of over 1,000,000. As such, these people are the upper echelon in the influencer community, but also have the highest fees (YouTube gamer DanTDM, (Dan Middleton), is one of the top compensated social media influencers, making approximately $16.5 million annually. He kicked off his YouTube career by focusing on daily Minecraft plays, and as his following grew, he expanded to other games.). The benefit is that mega-influencers have a variety of interests with diverse audiences, so they reach a lot of people, quite often, and as such, they often work with big brands with big marketing budgets.

So who are the big mega influencers? Take a look below at some of the top influencers in social media at the time of this writing.

1. As mentioned earlier, YouTube gamer DanTDM, (Dan Middleton), is one of the top compensated social media influencers, making approximately $16.5 million annually. He kicked off his YouTube career by focusing on daily Minecraft plays, and as his following grew, he expanded to other games.

2. Evan Fong of VanossGaming, makes approximately $15.5 million per year, just by playing video games and posting videos of his game play on YouTube.

3. Tyler Oakley, an LGBTQ activist, brings in $6 million per year through his videos on YouTube.
4. Kim Garst is a seasoned social selling professional, author and the co-founder of Boom! Social. While it is unknown how much she makes from her Twitter influence, she is a prolific tweeter and uses images often and well. Marketers are wise to make note of her strategies as part of their learning process.

As the number of followers changes on a daily basis, I intentionally haven't listed what they are as of the time of this writing. But, I do encourage you to take time to check out each of these influencers, whether you can afford to use them or not because it will give you visibility into how these celebrities approach the influencer marketing space.

So, let's now focus on how to find those influencers that are within your budget, now that you understand the various influencer tiers and the benefits of each.

There are a variety of platforms available to help you discover and engage with influencers that can positively help your brand. Key platforms include (but are not limited to) Upfluence, Buzzsumo, and HypeAuditor.

Each of these platforms comes with its own pros and cons, so be sure to review the platforms available and determine the one best for you, and for your budget. Also, as you grow awareness of your brand through your chosen social platforms, you may find influencers organically through followers who tend to comment on or share your content frequently. In these cases, and if they have a strong follower base (or a desire to grow it), consider sending these folks a direct message to start a conversation and to explore if they would want to become an influencer for you. Often these pre-nano-influencers can be enticed to become more of an informal influencer for you if you offer them a simple gesture of some kind, such as sending them a free product, gift card, or nominal one-time compensation.

CONCLUSION

Congratulations on making it this far! In conclusion, I would like to reemphasize why you must use social media marketing for your company:

1. Your customers are on social media
2. Social media marketing helps grow brand awareness and authority
3. Social media marketing will help you improve brand loyalty
4. Social media marketing grows inbound traffic (web visits and store/location visits)
5. Social media marketing allows you to target and retarget your customers and future customers
6. Social media marketing is much more cost-effective than more traditional channels
7. Social media marketing can help you improve your rankings with various search engines
8. Your competition is on social media
9. Social media marketing is proven to lead to increased conversation rates

10. Consumers like to see recommendations that are provided to them on social media

11. Social media marketing will help you grow your customer base

In this guide, my goal was to inform you, and ensure you were better equipped to develop a social media marketing strategy for your business. And I hope that I have achieved just that by introducing you to the basics of Facebook, YouTube, and Twitter, helping you to identify goals and objectives and set up your business profile, by helping you determine your niche, by providing you the tips and tricks to develop high-quality content, by helping you understand how to use hashtags and get new users, by educating you on how to pursue and leverage influencers, and by showing you the best time of day and the best day of the week to engage your followers.

If all of the above didn't stick, I hope that you'll read the book again, but also that you will in the least, take away a new respect and knowledge about the power of social media marketing. If you have decided for whatever reason that now is not the right time for you to start, I hope that you now have the tools you need, so that you can jumpstart the process when you determine you are ready.

CPSIA information can be obtained
at www.ICGtesting.com
Printed in the USA
BVHW041357100621
609275BV00006B/1494